Hampden C. DuBose

Preaching in Sinim

The Gospel to the gentiles, with hints and helps for addressing a heathen audience

Hampden C. DuBose
Preaching in Sinim
The Gospel to the gentiles, with hints and helps for addressing a heathen audience

ISBN/EAN: 9783337285692

Printed in Europe, USA, Canada, Australia, Japan

Cover: Foto ©Lupo / pixelio.de

More available books at **www.hansebooks.com**

Preaching in Sinim;

OR,

The Gospel to the Gentiles,

WITH

Hints and Helps for Addressing a Heathen Audience.

BY

Hampden C. DuBose, D. D.,

Twenty-one years a Missionary at Soochow,

Author of "The Dragon, Image and Demon; or, The Three Religions of China" (English); "The Street Chapel Pulpit" (Chinese); "An Illustrated Life of Christ with no Picture of our Lord" (Chinese), Etc., Etc.

"Knowing therefore the terror of the Lord, we persuade men."
"The love of Christ constraineth us."
"For I determined not to know anything among you, save Jesus Christ, and him crucified."

Richmond, Va.:
Presbyterian Committee of Publication.
1893.

COPYRIGHTED BY
JAS. K. HAZEN, *Sec'y of Presbyterian Committee of Publication.*
1893.

TO

MY BELOVED BRETHREN

OF THE

Southern Presbyterian Church,

WHO IN THEIR PULPITS

SO EARNESTLY AND ELOQUENTLY ADVOCATE

THE CAUSE OF

Foreign Missions,

THIS LITTLE TREATISE ON HOMILETICS IN CHINA IS

AFFECTIONATELY INSCRIBED.

PREFACE.

TO present the truth to those who have never heard the message of salvation in such a way that they may understand it, has been the single aim of my ministry in the land of Sinim. Especially during the preparation of the two hundred Street-Chapel sermons in Chinese was my attention called to this subject. The thoughts have been committed to writing with the desire that they might be of service to newly-arrived missionaries, and aid them in preaching to the heathen who know not God. It is also with the hope that some laborers in other lands might read these pages and *mutatis mutandis* adopt a few of the suggestions to the special wants of their fields.

As preaching is the great work of the Church of God, no doubt many of the friends of missions in the home-lands desire to know how those whom they send forth tell to the untutored pagan the new story of God's love, and we trust they will find these chapters satisfactory. Our great desire is that the young men in the colleges, whose attention is now turned to Eastern lands, may by reading be led to consecrate themselves to the work of preaching in China. In the eighteen provinces the four hundred millions need ten thousand missionaries immediately. May each one who hears the divine call, "Whom shall I send?" be enabled with the apostle to exclaim, "Unto me, who am the least of all saints, is this grace given, that I should preach among the Gentiles the unsearchable riches of Christ."

H. C. D.

Southern Presbyterian Mission, Soochow, China.

Note.—The MS. of *Preaching in Sinim* was placed in the hands of the Committee of Publication some two years since, but the issue of the volume has, for sufficient cause, been delayed.

CONTENTS.

	PAGE
CHAPTER I.	
THE GRANDEUR OF THE PULPIT,	9
CHAPTER II.	
SINIM'S CALL,	23
CHAPTER III.	
APOSTOLIC ACTION,	32
CHAPTER IV.	
THE STREET CHAPEL,	49
CHAPTER V.	
ITINERATION AND WOMAN'S WORK,	62
CHAPTER VI.	
THE SPIRITUAL KINGDOM,	71
CHAPTER VII.	
THE AMBASSADOR TO SINIM,	87
CHAPTER VIII.	
LITERARY PREPARATION,	97
CHAPTER IX.	
THE STYLE OF PREACHING,	109

CHAPTER X.
Natural Theology, ... 130

CHAPTER XI.
The Light of Ethics and the Darkness of Sin, ... 154

CHAPTER XII.
Preaching Christ, ... 169

CHAPTER XIII.
Jesus, the Model Preacher to the Heathen, . 190

CHAPTER XIV.
Paul the Preacher, ... 207

CHAPTER XV.
The Work of the Holy Spirit, . . . 219

CHAPTER XVI.
The Wonders of the Last Days, ... 229

CHAPTER XVII.
The Reaper and His Rewards, ... 237

PREACHING IN SINIM.

CHAPTER I.

THE GRANDEUR OF THE PULPIT.

THE propagation of Christianity by preaching stamps the gospel as divine. Eighteen hundred years ago, before ships traversed the mighty ocean, an Israelite, living within the narrow confines of Judea, brought up and educated in an uncultivated part of the land, and moving in the humble walks of life, conceived the grand idea of making Adam's guilty race the subjects of divine grace, and reclaiming the world from its atheism and polytheism, its superstition and idolatry, simply by preaching. Dead and buried at Jerusalem, and now "alive forevermore," a message was sent to his scattered disciples, "Behold, he goeth before you into Galilee; there shall ye see him," and eagerly they bent their footsteps towards the "mountain where Jesus had appointed them." There the resurrected Lord boldly declares, "All power is given unto me in heaven and in earth," an authority transcending all human claims, a majesty above all earthly glory, a dominion embracing all in heaven and in earth, "when he shall have put down all rule and all authority and power: for he must reign, till he hath put all enemies under his feet." The Mediatorial King, asserting his right to rule over kings and kingdoms, angels and archangels, heaven and earth, gave the order to take possession of the whole world in his name, pledging his omnipotence and omniscience to insure success. Because of this power given unto him he issues the commission, "Go ye, therefore, and teach all nations," to a "little flock," for the most part unlettered men, but who for three years enjoyed the instructions of their Lord, and who soon were to be "endued with power from on high." The command was not to go as Mahomet, with fire and sword, to propagate the new faith, or like Shakyamuni, with incense, candles and magical arts, but by mouth and voice to proclaim the unsearchable riches of Christ.

The Foolishness of Preaching.

Truly the words of the apostle seem appropriate, "For after that in the wisdom of God the world by wisdom knew not God, it pleased God by the foolishness of preaching to save them that believe. For the Jews require a sign, and the Greeks seek after wisdom: but we preach Christ crucified, unto the Jews a stumbling-block, and unto the Greeks foolishness; but unto them which are called, both Jews and Greeks, Christ the power of God, and the wisdom of God." In English-speaking countries the pulpit is honored; not so in ancient Greece and Rome, or ancient and modern China. Filling, as they do, the universe with gods, the thought that there is only one God is too simple a concept for the profound mind of the philosopher. Accustomed to their exalted views of human nature, how unlearned are our discourses about sin! With their lofty ideas concerning merit, how puerile seem our words about "filthy rags"! All their lives admiring altars adorned with fruits and flowers and fragrant with incense, how revolting the teaching of salvation by faith in a crucified Messiah! While they require God to furnish them with some visible sign of his existence, how empty seem our talks about an unseen Jehovah! Then, to attempt the overthrow of ancient religious institutions simply by preaching, appears so ignoble! Yea, to christianize three hundred and ninety millions by the oral communication of divine truth seems the height of folly. And when we speak of conversion by the supernatural influences of the Holy Spirit they consider us as demented enthusiasts, and cry as Festus, "Thou art beside thyself." We are to see our "calling" as preachers of the gospel; "God hath chosen the foolish things of the world to confound the wise; and God hath chosen the weak things of the world to confound the things which are mighty; and base things of the world, and things which are despised, hath God chosen, yea, and things which are not, to bring to nought things that are."

When Christ was about to call the dead to life, three of the evangelists record the fact that "they laughed him to scorn," so the whole plan of awakening nations sleeping the sleep of death, by the voice of living men trumpeting the gospel, is in contrast with human schemes. When Cæsar's dominion extended over Europe and Western Asia, for the man crucified by Roman authority to claim "all power," and with no arm of flesh to befriend his cause to send a scattered band of believers to go forth conquering and to conquer by the word of his power, seemed the height of folly; but as victory crowned their banner, so, nineteen hundred years after, may his messengers bear witness "unto the uttermost part of the earth," and rely upon the presence of the Master to give the word success.

The Glory of the Messenger.

Paul speaks of the "messengers of the churches and of the glory of Christ." Those who "labor in word and doctrine" are the messengers or ministers of the glory of Christ. The grandeur of the calling is summed up in the word "glory." From the beginning to the end of Revelation the highest conceptions of things, divine and eternal, are given to us under the term glory. The messenger is sent by one whose glory filleth the heavens, and of whom when on earth it was said, "We beheld his glory, the glory as of the only begotten of the Father." The missionary is to declare the glory of God among a people who glorify him not. He is the minister of a covenant of glory. "But if the ministration of death, written and engraven in stones was glorious, so that the children of Israel could not steadfastly behold the face of Moses for the glory of his countenance, which glory was to be done away, how shall not the ministration of the Spirit be rather glorious? For if the ministry of condemnation be glory, much more doth the ministration of righteousness excel in glory. For even that which was made glorious had no glory in this respect, by reason of the glory that excelleth. For if that which is done away is glorious, much more that which remaineth is glorious." The minister is to preach of him who was "received up into glory," and who, after he has guided us by his counsel, shall afterwards receive us to glory.

An Ambassador for Christ.

We are sent by Christ; we are equipped by Christ; we come for Christ; we are ambassadors for Christ. We do not receive our credentials from St. James or Washington, but are ministers plenipotentiary from the court of Heaven, sent with full authority from Jehovah to make a treaty with his rebellious subjects. We are to say, "Come now and let us reason together, saith the Lord." The man of God stands as a herald to make a proclamation of divine amnesty; as a preacher he teaches all things whatsoever Christ has commanded; as a minister he serves the people even as the Son of man came not to be ministered unto but to minister; as a shepherd he feeds the flock over which the Holy Ghost has made him an overseer; as an elder he rules in the house of God; as a star in the right hand of Him who walks in the midst of the golden candlesticks he shines with peculiar lustre.

THE MINISTER OF RECONCILIATION.

The apostle to the Gentiles distinctly sets forth the great business of the missionary: "God, who hath reconciled us to himself by Jesus Christ, and hath given to us the ministry of reconciliation; to-wit, that God was in Christ, reconciling the world unto himself, not imputing their trespasses unto them; and hath committed unto us the word of reconciliation. Now, then, we are ambassadors for Christ, as though God did beseech you by us; we pray you in Christ's stead, be ye reconciled to God." The reconciled sinner becomes the minister of reconciliation, and speaks the word of reconciliation. Just as Phinehas stood between the living and the dead, so, in a figure, we act as intermediaries, setting forth the reconciling love of the unseen God, and coming to men with the message,—we gently beseech you; we earnestly pray you; we humbly beg you—"Be ye reconciled."

NOT GIVEN TO ANGELS.

To proclaim his gospel the Lord chose men and not angels. This is one of the mysteries which men may desire to look into. The angels are pure; to them men would seem very vile. They dwell in light inaccessible and full of glory; this world would be very dark to them. Their appearance in the pulpit would dazzle the eyes, and it would be hard to restrain men from acts of worship. They have never been tempted and could have no sympathy with the Son of man, or the sons of men, as they pass through fiery trials. Having never sinned they know little of the redemption that is in Christ Jesus, and have never experienced the preciousness of forgiveness and the joys of conversion. It is given to man, who is conscious of his own weakness and shortcomings, to speak to his brother about the way by which he has been led to love and serve the Lord. Ministers not only preach the written word, but they preach the word which has filtered through the inner life of their spiritual consciousness, and thus are "manifestly declared to be the epistle of Christ," "written not with ink, but with the Spirit of the living God."

The Regions Beyond.

Paul rejoiced that he was called "to preach the gospel in the regions beyond, and not to boast in another man's line of things made ready to hand." "So that from Jerusalem, and round about Illyricum, I have fully preached the gospel of Christ. Yea, so have I strived to preach the gospel, not where Christ was named, lest I should build upon another man's foundation; but as it is written, To whom he was not spoken of, they shall see; and they that have not heard shall understand." In the home-land, with a pious ancestry, pious parents, pious families, pious friends, pious Sabbath-school teachers, pious pastors, pious churches, the air we breathe is "holiness to the Lord." Under such circumstances, the influence of a minister upon a new convert is reduced to the minimum, for many agencies (humanly speaking) have a share in bringing a soul to Christ. In the "field" which is "the world," the minister has few valuable colaborers in the work. Here it is the freshness of the salvation morn, with no gospel-hardened sinners to sit under the sound of the glad tidings, the dewdrops of grace glistening in the rising sun, and the joyful notes of sacred song for the first time wafted on the bracing air. There is a true romance of missions, the pioneer religious life in hoary lands of superstition, where, as our Lord could say, "Lift up your eyes, and look on the fields"—and what a sight!—"for they are white already to the harvest," like an Alabama cotton-field with its silken bolls so large and white, looking like a fall of snow in the autumn.

The Joy of Preaching.

The apostle said that he was "a debtor both to the Greeks and to the barbarians." There is a real pleasure in paying our debts. We often speak of the *duty* of obedience; there is no keener joy in the Christian life than obedience to God. In a heathen land we experience the preciousness of a nearness to God; the darkness around makes the light in the soul more appreciated. We talk of luxury; but is there any luxury like that of doing good? Philanthropy! the noblest form of oriental luxury. It is pleasant to carry the news of pardon to the prisoner in his chains; to tell "the old, old story" here, where it is the new, new theme. There is no possibility of its becoming a wearisome task. Hundreds of times the question has been put, "My friend, have you heard anything about the gospel?" "No." And the a-b-c of Christianity has been taught with as much exhilarating delight as if it were the first lesson to the first scholar. Sixteen days across the Pacific, on our return home, at nightfall the splendid steamship, *The City of Tokio*, stopped, and the passengers rushed on deck to see what was the matter. Directly a flash of light was seen from the Farral Islands, and, as the light revolved, another flash, and soon another; the whistle blew, the engines started, and soon we were within the Golden Gate. This was the first light from our native shore, and oh! what delight to all on board!

So it is joy without measure to tell for the first time the news of salvation to a benighted pagan.

Christian experience varies as do the lineaments of our faces, which not only differ in one age, but one generation is unlike another. Some find their sweetest moments in the closet; others, in the prayer-meeting; many consider their hours of reading the Scriptures the happiest; the sweet psalmists experience holy joy when singing the songs of Zion; while perhaps to a few the hour of preaching—the mind kindled to a white heat, and the heart directly under the influences of the Holy Spirit—brings the most vivid realization of God's presence, when he makes his goodness pass before his servant, and places him in a cleft of the rock, while his glory passeth by.

> Sweet hour to preach, sweet hour to preach,
> May I thy grace and glory reach,
> When on Mount Carmel's lofty height,
> I view false gods just in my sight,
> And call to men, Turn ye, and live;
> Here is the way, God's Son believe;
> And shout, while I can daily teach,
> Welcome, welcome, sweet hour to preach!

When leaving the chapel, and the footsteps are turned homeward, the messenger's feet fly swiftly along, the mind absorbed in celestial themes, the thought suddenly occurs: "Well, I am really here, walking on the earth."

What a beautiful couplet in the *Missionary Psalmody:*

> "Go ye, therefore, and teach all nations;
> And, lo! I am with you alway."

The presence of the Master is specially vouchsafed at the very moment when we teach the people to observe his commandments. If the chief attraction of heaven is to be "forever with the Lord," what on earth is better than the mission-field, with its daily preaching, and daily walks to Emmaus?

The Responsibility.

The apostolical evangelistic motto is: "Knowing, therefore, the terror of the Lord, we persuade men." Paul feared lest, when he had preached to others, he himself should be a castaway. As the soul is of more value than the body, so the responsibility resting upon winners of souls is a thousand-fold more weighty than that which lies upon those who deal with things temporal. The preacher is a watchman upon the towers of Zion. "If, when he seeth the sword come upon the land, he blow the trumpet, and warn the people, then whosoever heareth the sound of the trumpet, and taketh not warning, if the sword cometh and taketh him away, his blood shall be upon his own head. But he that taketh warning shall deliver his soul. But if the watchman see the sword come, and blow not the trumpet, and the people be not warned; if the sword come, and take any person away from them, he is taken away in his iniquity; but the blood will I require at the watchman's hands. So thou, O son of man, I have set thee a watchman unto the house of Israel; therefore thou shalt hear the word at my mouth, and warn them from me. When I say to the wicked, O wicked man, thou shalt surely die; if thou dost not speak to warn the wicked from his way, that wicked man shall die in his iniquity; but his blood will I require at thine hand. Nevertheless, if thou warn the wicked of his way, to turn him from it; if he do not turn from his way, he shall die in his iniquity; but thou hast delivered thy soul."

"Let Sion's watchmen all awake,
 And take the alarm they give;
Now let them from the mouth of God
 Their solemn charge receive.

"They watch for souls, for which the Lord
 Did heavenly bliss forego;
For souls which must forever live
 In raptures or in woe.

"All to the great tribunal haste,
　　The account to render there;
　And shouldst thou strictly mark our faults,
　　Lord, how should we appear?"

CHAPTER II.

Sinim's Call.

"UNTO you, O men, I call; and my voice is to the sons of men." It is a personal, direct, pressing summons, and requires immediate attention. "How then shall they call on him of whom they have not heard? and how shall they hear without a preacher?"

It is the call of a *great multitude*, even of 390,000,000. The vast wealth of William H. Vanderbilt was computed at his death: the dollars, if piled up, how high the column would reach; if spread out, how many square miles the silver would cover. Here there is a man for a coin, and a hundred million over!

It is a *wide* call: "Behold I set before you an open door." A half-century since the Middle Kingdom was compassed on every side by the great wall of seclusion. Thirty years ago foreigners were limited to the five open ports. The number has since increased to twenty. Now, by the toleration clause in the treaties, missionaries have the privilege of preaching in every part of the empire, and by the interpretation the Mandarins put upon the treaty, they may rent houses and live in the interior, and the officials grant them special protection. While the merchants are confined to residence in twenty localities, the ministers of the gospel are free to enter "the door great and effectual," which has been opened to the thousand walled cities, the one hundred thousand market towns, and the million villages, and everywhere proclaim salvation.

It is a *philanthropic* call. Says the royal preacher, "Withhold not good from them to whom it is due, when it is in the power of thine hand to do it." Is not the gospel good? Is it not the supreme good? Is it not due the heathen? Are we not debtors to the barbarians? Is it not in our power to give it? Does not the church send forth every man that offers? Shall we then withhold the bread of life from the famishing?

It is a *pointed* call. It does not generally come as a light from heaven, as in the case of Paul, or as a view of the throne as with Isaiah, or in audible words as with the child Samuel, but as a still small voice, "What doest thou here?" here in a gospel land, abounding in Bibles and preachers; here, where flows the water of life so freely; here, where whosoever will may be saved?

It is a *Macedonian* call. The apostle's biographer says, they "were forbidden of the Holy Ghost to preach the word in Asia," probably because so much work had been done there. "They assayed to go into Bithynia: but the Spirit suffered them not." At Troas "A vision appeared to Paul in the night: there stood a man of Macedonia, and prayed him, saying, Come over into Macedonia, and help us. And after he had seen the vision, immediately we endeavoured to go into Macedonia, assuredly gathering that the Lord had called us for to preach the gospel unto them."

It is a call which requires *obedience:* "Whatsoever he saith unto you do it." Does the Master say, "Go ye into all the world"? then the presumption is, that the field of labor assigned the one who is called to preach is beyond the limits of his own country, and before he concludes to remain he should seek a clear call to stay at home.

It is a *divine* call: "Pray ye therefore the Lord of the harvest, that he will send forth laborers into his harvest." It seems that the disciples did pray, for immediately follows the roll of the twelve whom Jesus "called." The evangelists give the simple narrative how Christ called his disciples one by one. He said, "Follow Me." He is the great Captain of the sacramental host that goes forth to the peoples which "sit in darkness and in the region and shadow of death." "And no man taketh this honour unto himself but he that is called of God."

It is a call *from the Holy Ghost*. The anointing of the Spirit is an essential prerequisite. At the first missionary meeting at Antioch, when the apostles and elders were assembled together, "As they ministered unto the Lord and fasted, the Holy Spirit said, Separate me Barnabas and Saul for the work whereunto I have called them." When the designation to the sacred office comes from the third person of the adorable Trinity it may be said, "For he is a chosen vessel unto me, to bear my name before the Gentiles and kings and the children of Israel."

The call is both external and internal. It is external in the leadings of Providence, which open the way to heathen nations and which remove the obstacles from the path of the one appointed. It is external in the approbation of the church and in the laying on of hands, by which the candidate is set apart to the sacred office. It is internal in that the man by prayer and the study of God's word feels prompted to go and teach the benighted nations. As an aged minister said to me when I was at the Theological Seminary, "If the Lord puts it into your heart to go, why go." When the party who feels the internal call receives the approbation of God's people, there is evidence that he is called of God.

It is a call for *volunteers:* "And I heard the voice of the Lord, saying, Whom shall I send, who will go for us? Then said I, Here am I; send me." Our Master was an illustrious example of a living sacrifice. "And he saw that there was no man, and wondered that there was no intercessor: therefore his arm brought salvation unto him." "Wherefore, when he cometh into the world, he saith, Sacrifice and offering thou wouldst not, but a body hast thou prepared me. Then said I, Lo, I come (in the volume of the book it is written of me) to do thy will, O God." No church forcibly sends a man to the mission field; he must volunteer.

It is a *glowing* call. A yearning to lead the most useful life during our few years upon the earth, a hungering and thirsting to preach he word to the heathen, a burning of the heart, within as we walk with Jesus and hear his last great command. Into it enter all the elements of the higher Christian life; love for Jesus, compassion for the helpless, zeal for the Master's glory, obedience to his commands, and joy in carrying the word to earth's remotest end.

It is a *growing* call. When I was taken under the care of Presbytery a venerable preacher asked, "Do you feel, 'Yea, woe is me if I preach not the gospel'?" The answer was, "I do not," but three years afterwards the meaning of the words was a matter of personal experience. When the sinner is called to Christ he does not care to come till he feels his need, so no one desires to come to the foreign field till he realizes the needs of the heathen. This is developed by the study of what the Bible says about idolatry, of the promises in reference to the kingdom, and of the missionary journeys of the apostles. The study of geography and of the comparative civilizations and the religions of the heathen awaken the slumbering call. Missionary literature opens a wide field for investigation, and leads the inquirer to personal consecration. Were there a large heathen city just across the river, would not many desire to labor within its walls, and is not time and distance annihilated by the great ships which now traverse the ocean? As we strive to grow in every Christian grace, let the young see they neglect not to cultivate the call to Foreign

Missions, chiefly by prayer and communion with God. All learning is useful, especially as the opportunities for mental improvement in the field are limited, but as a long literary curriculum is necessary in learning the language, any man of ordinary ability, after a brief theological and thorough Biblical course, may, under the blessing of God, become eminently useful. The qualifications of a Sabbath-school teacher are those especially needed by missionaries who teach the pagan.

The lines written by Rev. Dr. Nathan Brown find an echo in many a heart. The only time it was the writer's privilege to meet him was at a social prayer-meeting at his home, and the stranger invited to speak mentioned how widely "The Missionary's Call" had been copied, and placed it beside Bishop Heber's

"From Greenland's Icy Mountains,"

as a part of the missionary heritage. Dr. Brown was requested by one present to give the history of the poem, and he said it was the first time he had ever been asked to do so. Written at the age of nineteen, when he was at college, it was sent to a newspaper, but hearing nothing from it he was discouraged as to further attempts to reach the heathen field, and went to the printer's trade. Afterwards he saw it copied in a Princeton magazine, and this held out some hope. After a lapse of time it was printed in the Baptist papers, and (though he did not say so), the Society sought him out. He lived 3x19 years to to preach in Assam and Japan.

> "My soul is not at rest: there comes a strange
> And secret whisper to my spirit, like
> A dream at night, which tells me I am on
> Enchanted ground. Why live I here? The vows
> Of God are on me, and I may not stop
> To play with shadows, or pluck earthly flowers,
> Till I my work have done and rendered up
> Account. The voice of my departed Lord,
> 'Go teach all nations,' from the Eastern world
> Comes on the night air and awakes my ear.
>
> "And I will go. I may no longer doubt
> To give up friends, and home, and idle hopes,
> And every tender tie that binds my heart
> To thee, my country. Why should I regard
> Earth's little store of borrowed sweets?
> . . . . Never was it his design
> Who placed me here that I should live at ease
> Or drink at pleasure's fountain. Henceforth, then,
> It matters not if storm or sunshine be
> My earthly lot, bitter or sweet my cup:
> I only pray, God fit me for the work;
> God make me holy and my spirit nerve

For the stern hour of strife.   Let me but know
There is an arm unseen that holds me up,
An eye that kindly watches all my path,
Till I my weary pilgrimage have done ;
Let me but know I have a friend that waits
To welcome me to glory, and I joy
To tread the dark and death fraught wilderness."

CHAPTER III.

Apostolic Action.

THE eloquent Athenian, when asked, "What is the chief element in oratory, answered, "Action." "And what is the second?" "Action." "And what the third?" "Action." The same might be said of apostolic evangelization. There is need of Action, Action, Action. Our Master calls attention to the wisdom of the children of this world, and the energy they display in their generation. For instance, go into a native store in this city, and see the prints, a hundred different patterns, prepared in Europe to suit the Chinese eye and taste. How the consuls at the foreign ports watch trade, and keep their respective governments informed of every available opening! In all departments of business throughout the world the most intense activity is displayed. This is the example which our Lord sets before the children of light in the evangelization of the nations.

We do not find Christ sitting in the temple at Jerusalem, or building a tabernacle in the metropolis, and summoning all Judea and the region round about Jordan to come and sit at his feet, for it is recorded, "He went about doing good." After he had preached in the synagogue at Capernaum, the people "sought him, and came unto him, and stayed him, that he should not depart from them. And he said unto them, I must preach the kingdom of God to other cities also, for therefore am I sent." Constant activity, unceasing labors, and unremitting exertions marked the daily life of our Lord; so, if we are hereafter to share in his glory, we must now share in his toil. Blessed privilege, to be co-workers with God!

The apostle to the Gentiles, in speaking of his work, could say: "I labored more abundantly than they all." Doctor Charles Hodge says: "This may mean either more than any one of the apostles, or more than all of them put together. The latter is more in keeping with the tone of the passage. It serves more to exalt the grace of God; and it is historically true, if the New Testament record is to be our guide." In the great work of converting the world the labors of the apostle are placed before us in a formidable array. Are we followers of Paul, as he followed Christ? It is not a safe method to count the laborers, numbering one by one; for though all are members of the same body, yet all are not of the same relative importance, as what is the utility of the little finger, compared to that of the eye?

A fearful responsibility rests upon the foreign evangelist because of his independent position. He has no congregation upon whom he is financially dependent, and who make vigorous demands on the pulpit and the pastorate. The home society is across the sea, and takes only a general oversight of the work. He preaches as often as he desires, and itinerates whenever he chooses, so his stay in the city or country is according to his own will. As in ancient Israel, "every man doeth as is right in his own eyes." Truly, our Lord has gone on a long journey, and the preparation for his return is the great object before the missionary in all his labors.

The field is the world, but China is specially the field for preaching. By treaty-right, we may go from province to province, and from city to city, and proclaim salvation; and here almost is fulfilled the vision of John: "And I saw another angel fly in the midst of heaven, having the everlasting gospel to preach unto them that dwell on the earth." Throughout Christendom it is considered that the minister's duties fall chiefly on Sunday, but here it is different, for every day is a day of preaching, and, freed from heavy pastoral labor, after three years of language study one is as free as the birds of the air to make known the glad tidings of salvation.

There is a pleasant variety in evangelistic methods. In one sense, continued preaching is a weariness to the flesh, as spiritual labor is so much harder than manual. On the other hand, it may be considered light work. To be out of doors, free from books and teachers, going from place to place, taking active exercise, and breathing the pure air of heaven, is wonderfully invigorating to both the physical and spiritual man. In the chapels, when too tired to preach longer, we may sit down on a bench and engage in conversation; or, if we become weary at this, we may pass from shop to shop when, in the unoccupied portions of the day, the dozen clerks leaning upon the counter are glad to have some one to converse with. Or to vary the scene, we may step into a tea-shop, sip a cup of tea, and converse with the ten, twenty, or thirty who gather around. If the voice is tired, it may be rested by colportage. If suffering with bronchitis, we may pass from house to house, distribute leaflets, or mount posters and gospel proclamations on the walls. When the city work becomes monotonous, the country, with its green fields, is open, and the courteous peasants will bring out a bench, offer a cup of tea, and press the visitor to stay and preach.

One element in successful missionary work is *punctuality*. When the clock points the hour, let the man of God go forth to his daily task. There are many interruptions incidental to missionary life,—Chinese visitors who call, converts coming for instruction, native ministers who wish to consult, the general oversight of the mission to be taken,—but if on some day there is only one and one-half hours, and it takes one-half hour to walk to the chapel and one-half hour to return, let the other thirty minutes be given to public preaching. Punctuality in a minister is a cardinal Christian virtue.

Another element is *saving time*. "Redeeming the time" is the Scripture phraseology. Much of our time is, as it were, locked up in the musty store-rooms of a pawn shop. It must be redeemed. "Slowly, slowly go," is the Chinaman's motto; "Diligent in business" is the Christian's rule of life. The apostle says, "And we desire that every one of you do shew the same diligence . . . unto the end, that ye be not slothful." Itinerating in this well-watered region, by voyaging at night we may redeem the days for labor. The preciousness of time must be ever prominently and intently before the child of God. Dr. Baccus, of Baltimore, was noted for his efficient pastorate. It is said that if he had ten minutes to spare before an appointment he would step out and call on a parishioner.

A third element is *to make a business of preaching*, just as the merchant at his store, or the lawyer at his office. And here is the great besetting sin to which the preacher of the gospel is exposed; that is, to do this spiritual work in a professional way; still, according to the parable of the two sons, it is better to go in a wrong spirit than not to go at all, for in the act of obedience we are in the line of receiving the blessing. The claims of flesh and blood—mail day, family cares, times of social intercourse—must not interfere with our one great object of being preachers of righteousness. It must not be light work; it must be our life-work. The hand of the diligent in spiritual as well as temporal things, maketh rich. "Seest thou a man diligent in his business," says the royal preacher, "he shall stand before kings." The missionary must be a hard-working man. There is nothing that makes more impression upon a Mongolian, traveling in the "old stage coach," than activity and enterprise.

Along with this, the man of God has a holy horror of the sin of laziness. Is it not to be classed with idolatry? There sits the idol with the hollow of his feet turned heavenward, but not so the heaven-sent messenger. Paul was called to preach; but the call was so glorious he lay flat upon his back. What a picture of a man appalled at the magnitude of the task of bringing a nation to Christ. The command was given, "Rise, and stand upon thy feet." Then was delivered unto him the great missionary commission: "I have appeared unto thee for this purpose, to make thee a minister and a witness both of these things which thou hast seen, and of those things in the which I will appear unto thee; delivering thee from the people, and from the Gentiles, unto whom now I send thee, to open their eyes, and to turn them from darkness to light, and from the power of Satan unto God, that they may receive forgiveness of sins, and inheritance among them which are sanctified by faith that is in me." Paul repeated the charge to his son Timothy: "I charge thee therefore before God, and the Lord Jesus Christ, who shall judge the quick and the dead at his appearing and his kingdom; preach the word; be instant in season, out of season; reprove, rebuke, exhort with all long-suffering and doctrine. . . . . Watch thou in all things, endure afflictions, do the work of an evangelist, make full proof of thy ministry."

In the fifth place, we must, as far as in us lies, keep our bodies in trim for preaching, and do nothing that would interfere with our duties as speakers. The athlete looking forward to the games keeps his limbs in training. If study unfits one for the great aim of life, the time out of the pulpit must be spent in buoyant recreation, enjoyable reading, or pleasant visiting. The health and vigor of the body is a prime factor in arduous labors. The work reacts on the man, and there is no surer panacea for headache or languor than an attack on idolatry.

Prime attention must also be given to keeping the mind bright by sharpening the axe on some literary grindstone. In the interior, separated from the great Western world, dullness is apt to creep over our intellects, and unfit us for our avocation. Though in the old country, we are in a new world of intellectual enterprise, so there is no necessity for mental torpor. It should be our effort to consecrate every talent to the Master's service.

Again, the gospel messenger must not spend his time in his study. It would be like a courier from the capital loitering at an inn. Dr. Knowlton, of precious memory, says: "The command of Christ, and the nature and necessities of the work, demand that missionaries maintain the campaign in the field against the enemy, and not spend their time in more congenial pursuits than the rugged contact with the heathen in preaching. The great Captain has given them strict orders to preach his gospel, and they are not at liberty to neglect this work for any other. What would we say of an ambassador to a foreign court, who, instead of devoting himself exclusively to the interest of the government by which he is commissioned, should spend his time in literary pursuits, or devote himself to trade, or entangle himself in the political affairs of the government to which he is sent? And how can a missionary answer to him who gave him his commission, if he does not devote himself to the explicit business that was entrusted to him?" We are to mingle with the people, become friendly with them and know them intimately. Of our Lord it was said, "The Word was made flesh and dwelt among us." During the snows of winter and the summer suns we may bring our barks into port and mend our tattered sails. "As we have, therefore, opportunity let us do good unto all men."

Literary work seems to open a wide field of usefulness, and some may think: "Write a volume, and it will be read by millions; preaching is evanescent, but a book endures for generations!" There is no more fallacious form of reasoning. Only a small percentage of the people can read. The eyes of those who do read the written page often merely run down the lines of characters without thinking of the meaning. It must, too, be remembered that spoken words live for centuries in their effects upon the minds and hearts of men. Also, only those books which are evolved from the energizing power of an active ministry are likely to be practical and useful. Yet we are not to underrate the labors of the great students who have prepared the text-books in language and literature, by the use of which we have been qualified for our great work. The church needs a few of her mighty men in the quiet retirement of their studies, with time for meditation, to prepare the great books which mould the minds of men. By their writings they preach to many. Division commanders are often at their headquarters in the rear, removed from the scene of actual conflict, and from thence control the movements of their troops. The major-generals direct the forces, but the rank and file of the missionary corps must go into the enemy's camp, and wield the sword of the Spirit.

The doctrine of justification by faith is so precious to the church that the Christian is prone to forget that faith must be shown by works, as the Apostle James so pointedly correlates the centrifugal and centripetal forces of salvation: "But wilt thou know, O vain man, that faith without works is dead? Was not Abraham, our father, justified by works, when he had offered Isaac, his son, upon the altar? Seest thou how faith wrought with his works, and by works was faith made perfect? And the Scripture was fulfilled which saith, Abraham believed God, and it was imputed unto him for righteousness." It is by zeal in preaching that there is proof of faith in the Lord who gave the command to preach. To the railway, steam without the engine evaporates, and the engine without steam is motionless; so to the minister, preaching without faith is powerless, and faith without preaching is vacuity. Of our Saviour it was said, he "was clad with zeal as a cloak"; "for the zeal of thine house hath eaten me up"; "my zeal hath consumed me." It was not simply a fervent, glowing zeal, but a consuming zeal. The foreign evangelist is "to give himself wholly to prayer and the ministry of the word." Along with his prayers, faith, fastings, and reliance upon the power of the Holy Spirit, must be the active work of the body to prove that the spiritual soul is alive. Do we read the life of Christ, and behold his mighty deeds of power and love? Our Lord himself said: "And greater works than these shall he do;" referring, perhaps, not so much to his miracles as to the disciples uniting with him in seeking and saving the lost, and in proclaiming the truth, not in one little country, but throughout the earth. In the parable of the body and its members, the apostle charges believers not to judge of the usefulness of others: "But now hath God set the members every one of them in the body, as it hath pleased him. . . . Nay, much more those members of the body, which seem to be more feeble, are necessary."

Our labors must be unremitting. Before Jericho, "The seven priests bearing seven trumpets of rams' horns before the ark of the Lord went on continually, and blew with the trumpets." This seemed a very foolish method. Why not take a few thousand braves and make a breach in the wall? The priests blew, and blew, and blew. The Bible puts the trumpet as the symbol of the ministry, and the blowing of the trumpet as the preaching of the word. Our Saviour's instructions are two-fold; that the disciple have girded loins and burning lights. How important to the Chinese garments is the girdle, and to Elijah I. and Elijah II. a "leathern girdle" was appropriate. The minister's light must be burning and shining, as John's camp-fire in the wilderness of Judea. It has been said of a venerable lady, whose bow still abides in strength and whose active labors have been richly blessed, that her life is summed up in the word "Go." President Lincoln wittily said of a famous General, "He is an admirable engineer, but he seems to have a special talent for a *stationary engine.*" Before General Grant, whom success seemed always to attend, took command of the army of the Potomac, and when Stonewall Jackson, the God-fearing and Sabbath-keeping chieftain, was making his rapid marches, and, by his sudden advances, placing a double line of pickets in front and attacking the rear, with 13,000 successively defeating three Generals whose combined armies (which were never suffered to combine) numbered 60,000, General Halleck, under date of October 7, 1862, wrote: "There is a decided want of legs in our army." May the multitudes who dwell within the walls of China, like the people of Jehovah at the gates of Jerusalem, who watched the messengers of mercy descending the Mount of

Olives, exclaim: "How beautiful are the feet of them that preach the gospel of peace, and bring glad tidings of good things." The heralds of salvation must be Alexanders in their wide marches, and Napoleons in their impetuous onslaughts.

The Saviour's command is to bear *much fruit*. A tree is known by its fruits, and is prized for its fine large crop. How, some years, the vines which twine around our verandahs are borne down by the heavy clusters; not one grape here and another there, but, as the Chinese say, "Globes of fruit." Let the *preach* tree bear much fruit. "So," says Jesus, "shall ye be my disciples." Trees of the Lord's planting, whose branches bend beneath the weight of the rich golden fruit. Our Master says, "Thou shalt love the Lord thy God with all thy heart, and with all thy soul, and with all thy mind, and with all thy strength." Also, "If ye love me, keep my commandments." My command is to preach, therefore preach "with all thy heart, and with all thy soul, and with all thy mind, and with all thy strength." When past fourscore, it is recorded of John Wesley, "Every day his voice is still heard somewhere sounding the alarm at five o'clock in the morning. Nearly every evening the sun goes down upon him in some other place. He has chapels scattered over the whole country, but he still, almost daily, proclaims his message in the fields and on the highways." On the 1st of January, 1790, when eighty-five, he wrote, "I am now an old man, decayed from head to foot. However, blessed be God, I do not slack my labor. I can preach still." In the midst of formalism and church inertia in England arose this great spiritual man, who preached several times each day, and success marked his labors. Amidst the deadness of Chinese systems missionaries have the golden opportunity to show forth the glory of preaching. Just as a native said of a faithful Wesleyan in this land, "Whenever you meet him he talks about Jesus."

> "Take the name of Jesus with you,
> Child of sorrow and of woe;
> It will joy and comfort give you,
> Take it then where'er you go.
> Precious name, O how sweet,
> Hope of earth and joy of heaven."

There are so few men we must multiply ourselves. It is not $x + y$ but $(x + y)^2$. A division of labor is often spoken of; that is not the question; it is a multiplication of labor. The Chinese rotate their crops, but it is not corn this year and cotton the next, but rice and wheat, and beans and vegetables, from the same land within one twelvemonth. The more one does, the more he has the ability to do; the strength increases with the increasing endeavors. Just as the muscles improve by training, so the missionary athlete, year by year, has more facility in his work. The heart expands, the feet grow nimble, the hands more skilled, the voice better trained. "In the morning sow thy seed, and in the evening withhold not thy hand; for thou knowest not whether shall prosper, either this or that, or whether they both shall be alike good." In the parable of the pounds, to each servant was given one pound. Said one, "Lord, thy pound hath gained ten pounds," or 1000 per cent! He was appointed to a prefecture.

A special blessing is promised to those who, like Caleb, *wholly follow* the Lord; and the young warrior who could say, "Let us go up and occupy the land, for we are abundantly able to overcome it," could at fourscore, when coming to claim the promise, exclaim, "As my strength was then, so is my strength now, for war, both to go out and come in." To his eye a walled city was no more than a mud fort. Look at the fifteen hundred missionaries!—twelve to one of the disciples in the upper chamber at Jerusalem. "To them is accorded the high honor of making known the gospel to the millions." The salvation army comes not with drum, and fife, and gong, but with the sweet notes of invitation, "Come unto me all ye that labor." The true crusaders are leading the consecrated host through the narrow passes of Asia to the Jerusalem above.

"But this I say, brethren, the time is short." We may have ten springs in which to sow our seed, or twenty summers when Apollos may pump water on the fields, or thirty autumns to gather the golden grain, or, by reason of strength, forty winters preparing for those who are to enter into our labors, yet our lives are but as a shadow which fleeth away. "Whatsoever thy hand findeth to do, do it with thy might; for there is no work, nor device, nor knowledge, nor wisdom in the grave, whither thou goest."

> "Work for the night is coming,
>   Work through the morning hours,
> Work while the dew is sparkling,
>   Work 'mid springing flowers ;
> Work when the day grows brighter,
>   Work in the glowing sun,
> Work, for the night is coming,
>   When man's work is done."

CHAPTER IV.

THE STREET CHAPEL.

THE Saviour's ascension command is not limited to clime or place. In Japan theatres are often rented by the native Christians, and one thousand Japanese will patiently sit, their pipe and rice beside them, for five or six hours, and listen to several speakers advocate the claims of Christianity. Also "preaching-places" are established, and become the nuclei of churches. In India, public preaching is held in the bazars of the great cities. In China, the principal place is the street chapel. The hall for preaching may be described as a part of the street cut off and enclosed, or a combination of the church and the highroad of travel. This is a biblical institution : "And Paul dwelt two whole years in his own hired house, and received all that came unto him, preaching the kingdom of God, and teaching those things which concern the Lord Jesus Christ with all confidence, no man forbidding him."

Its advantages are : 1, It secures punctuality on the part of the minister. 2, It becomes known as a central place for preaching, and by its permanency influences a people who are influenced by perennial institutions. "A city that is set on a hill cannot be hid." 3, The hearers are impressed with the sanctity of God's house. 4, When seated, they will listen twice as long as if standing on the street. 5, Inquirers may quietly sit and ask questions. 6, There are opportunities for prayer: "Is it not written, My house shall be called of all nations the house of prayer?" 7, It is the hub around which the wheel of itineration revolves.

Chapels should be situated on the most prominent streets of the city. Rents may be high, and lots sold by the front foot, but these items should not enter into the calculation. If the missionary's salary is $1,000, why not give him $500 more as rent for a chapel, if it will place his influence at the maximum? It is the price of the horse and the cart together, not taken separately. Again, if the moneys spent in travelling, in the three years at the language, and in furloughs, be considered, the church is at great expense in maintaining the missionary, and it should be used in the most effective way possible. Another thought is, that the man sacrifices his life for the gospel's sake, and he ought to be so situated that the highest good might be accomplished. Three thousand or five thousand dollars spent on a lot would be a permanent investment for the mission till the land was evangelized. As a practical matter, good houses may be rented for $100 a year, or one purchased for $1,000, in most of our cities. The street chapel is for the heathen; churches where Christians assemble for worship on the Sabbath should be in quiet localities, and ought to be built with Chinese silver. To the millions we should cry, "Buy wine and milk, without money and without price," on the first streets of the metropolis.

The building, constructed in the style of native halls, should be large, and accessible to the sunlight, so that it may be well ventilated when there is no service. To secure large audiences, stoves in winter, and *punkas* in summer, may be successfully introduced. The doors should be large, or the entire front removed, as with the native shops. It disarms prejudice, and the Chinese like it. I once preached in a large chapel on a very good street to an audience of five. The door was small, and there was a screen-door within, and the passers-by never noticed that there was preaching. A few masons to knock out the end of the building would have remedied the evil. The benches should be four or five feet apart. A Chinaman takes his seat on the end, and as, in winter, he has on many layers of cotton-padded clothing, he effectually bars the way; and so, if the forms are crowded, there will be only one man to a pew. It was remarked by a friend: "I cannot get the people to sit in my chapel;" and the suggestion was made, "Remove two out of three of your benches." The hint was taken, and no difficulty was afterwards experienced on this point. It is of the utmost importance to require the people to be seated, as it increases vastly their respect for the house of God.

The invitation is to "all that pass by." The open doors, like unto the gates of the celestial city, which "shall not be shut at all by day," bespeak a welcome. The voice of song attracts attention. Twenty or thirty are present. Prayer is offered. Men know they have not come to a theatre, but to a solemn assembly. The speaker commences, and all eyes are fixed upon him. He warms up in his subject, and soon the vacant sittings are filled, and fifty or a hundred are giving ear to the word. The attention is unwearied. Here sits the countryman, resting on his journey; the artisan, who wishes to know something of this strange cult; the clerk, who likes to hear the foreigner speak his own language; the merchant from a distant province; the passing traveller, with only five minutes to sit, and the mandarin's assistant, wishing to while away an hour; the coolie in his sandals, and the gentleman robed in satin; the old woman who goes to the temple to worship, and the scholar, full of pride and prejudice, armed against the teachers and teachings of Christianity. Some are attracted by the foreigner's appearance, many come to listen to illustrations and allegories, and others, simply because they have nothing better to do. Some listen as to a lecture on a literary theme, others seek for something better than the religions they possess.

The Chinese, though an industrious people, are not busy like their Western antipodes, so they have time to watch a sparrow on the roof, or to assemble, like the sons of Heth at the cave of Machpelah, to witness an important transaction, so they have leisure to come to the chapels during the day. The congregation is composed of a succession of those who come in and pass out. At the sound of the mandarin's gong, or the music preceding a bride or a coffin, a large number suddenly go to the door, but a hymn fills the vacated seats, and the foreigner and native, each taking turns two or three times, have addressed the two hundred or five hundred who have entered the sacred courts. Some days the audience is restless, as at the feasts, but on others, they sit as if riveted to the spot, and give the most serious attention. At times the speaker is electrified by the fixedness of the gaze of a whole congregation. There is no sphere where tact is so much needed as when the audience is fluctuating. Sometimes, when the preacher reaches "fifthly," those who heard the first point have retired and others have taken their places. The mode of address is not so much one long sermon as a series of short ones, resembling on a narrow-guage railway a train of little coaches coupled together.

The street chapel is the missionary's fort, where he throws hot shot and shell into the enemy's camp; the citadel, where he defends the truth; the school, where he teaches the A, B, C of heaven; the home, where he loves to dwell; the altar, upon which he is laid a living sacrifice; the church, in which he worships; the throne, on which he rules the minds and hearts of the heathen; the happy land, where he enjoys communion with his Maker; the hill of Zion, where he sings sweet songs; the gate of heaven, where the angels ascend and descend. There are special promises to these earthly tabernacles filled with the glory of Jehovah: "Thy way, O God, is in the sanctuary." Where is it that revivals have occurred and souls have been converted?

Is not God's way of salvation in the sanctuary? The Bible constantly mentions how specially Jehovah delights in the families of his people, but the sweet Psalmist says: "The Lord loveth the gates of Zion more than all the dwellings of Jacob." "And of Zion it shall be said, This and that man was born in her: and the highest himself shall establish her. The Lord shall count, when he writeth up his people, that this man was born there." "Who hath despised the day of small things?" "This is the word of the Lord . . . Not by might, nor by power, but by my Spirit, saith the Lord of hosts." "Who art thou, O great mountain" of idolatry? Before the street chapel "thou shalt become a plain, and he shall bring forth the headstone thereof with shoutings, crying, Grace, grace, unto it."

The audiences are made up of men from many provinces. We always bid them, "When you go home, 'Let him that heareth say, Come.'" In all the adjoining cities, as soon as the foreigner goes on shore, he is immediately recognized, and called by the name of the chapel. The very church, with its open doors and voice of free grace, becomes a mighty agency for bringing Christianity to the notice of the people. At home a town may be moved by a revival service of three or four weeks, but here these great cities need a protracted meeting of three or four centuries.

The minister should aim at immediate conversions, and it is essential to have a room attached to the chapel for prayer and conversation, to which men are invited, and where they may receive more particular instruction. It is the special duty of the fishers of men to be keenly alive to seeking out the more hopeful cases, and no efforts should be spared to bring the party without delay to confess his sins, believe in Christ, and receive baptism. A chapel without prayer is a field with her hedges all broken down. The Master preached to vast multitudes, and afterwards withdrew to communion with his chosen few. He who spoke to the five thousand in the wilderness afterwards preached to the one at the well. All great evangelists, after they have ministered to the great assembly, hold special converse with those who retire to the inquiry-room. The way to obtain the "hopeful few" is by preaching to the many. To get a little cream we must have a quantity of milk. Preaching to the multitudes, and making special efforts for the few, are supplementary. The question, however, is not whether it is better to preach to the many, or to speak individually to the few, but that of systematic, persistent efforts to make known the gospel.

The inquiry is sometimes made, "How often shall we preach?" Do we ask the question, "How often shall we eat?" In one place the morning is the time to reach the countrymen, and sow the seed in drills; in another, the afternoon affords the finest opportunity for broadcasting the grain; while at night, when the neighbors gather together and listen so solemnly, the missionary realizes, "He that goeth forth and weepeth, bearing precious seed, shall doubtless come again with rejoicing, bringing his sheaves with him." It is the speaker who uses his voice one day a week, not seven, who suffers with clergyman's sore throat.

Some may prefer an office, or a large reception-room, upon a prominent street, with glass doors hung on patent hinges, which open with a PUSH, where the fire burns brightly in the grate, and the missionary can sit a long time teaching the law of God to those who come in. The effectiveness of work depends more upon the number of hours a day given to religious teaching than upon the size of the chapel. In connection with the chapel there should also be a reading-room and book-stall well supplied with Christian and scientific literature. No pains should be spared in making the place attractive.

To reach the masses the most effective way is by the street chapel. During the course of twenty years, one million men may come into a chapel daily opened, and hear something of the plan of salvation. It is the Master's scheme for leavening a great lump: "So is the kingdom of God, as if a man should cast seed into the ground; and should sleep, and rise night and day, and the seed should spring and grow up, he knoweth not how. For the earth bringeth forth fruit of herself; first the blade, then the ear, after that the full corn in the ear. But when the fruit is brought forth, immediately he putteth in the sickle, because the harvest is come." As a pious naval officer looked from the top of the pagoda at the millions within view, and his attention was called to the feeble band trying to evangelize the plain, he said: "It must be discouraging, it must be discouraging." The answer was made: "Not at all; the government does not expect your flagship to conquer the world; you are simply to go where you are ordered, and do your duty."

To reach the same men over and over again there is no method like the street chapel. As it is a public resort for all classes and conditions of men, if a man's heart is touched he is likely to come whenever he has opportunity. Hundreds of faces are as familiar as the regular attendants at a home church. All throughout the country round about, men will say, "I have heard preaching many tens of times."

As a civilizing agency the street chapel is prominent. The root of opposition to Western institutions is prejudice. The daily association of a missionary with hundreds gradually dislodges these prepossessions and makes a breach into the wall of Chinese obstructiveness. Just as King James's version has exercised a most conservative effect on English literature, or as the American pulpit is a most powerful element in the education of the masses, so the incidental effect of the street chapel is elevating, and that in a very marked degree.

The chapel is an enlightening agency. Its great effect is seen in the diffusion of the truth. "For God, who commanded the light to shine out of darkness, hath shined in our hearts, to give the light of the knowledge of the glory of God." After a chapel has been opened for a number of years in a centre, if we go one hundred miles away we will mark the difference in the amount of general knowledge about Christianity the people possess. The *enlightenment* of the multitude is a great object in missionary labor.

It is a converting agency. When the oldest chapel now in this city was first opened, three men immediately professed the faith. Since then, one and another in the city and in the country have been brought in. A man in Peking, uniting with a church of another denomination, said that he first heard the gospel in a Soochow chapel. The preacher who first arrests the attention of a carnal pagan to spiritual things is, in a figure, his spiritual father. One who, for thirty years, has done chapel preaching in the central metropolis of the Flowery Kingdom writes: "There is scarcely a communion Sunday, from one end of the year to the other, on which some are not admitted into the church by baptism. Last year more than a hundred adults were admitted into our fellowship."

We come, as John the Baptist, to prepare the way for the descent of the Holy Ghost,—the seed must first be sown, then cometh the rain. There are three departments of knowledge which precede regeneration—the knowledge of God, the knowledge of sin, and the knowledge of Christ's death. While reasoning on these topics, the minister is kept in lively expectation and earnestly looking for the glorious appearing of the

Lord at his second coming, and with brightest hopes for the judgment of the great King, when all the streams of influence will be traced from their source to where they empty into the great ocean of eternity. The street chapel will then shine with the brightness of the firmament. Results are not to be estimated by the annual number of converts, for we do not labor by the day, or the month, or the year. We are to preach the gospel of the kingdom in all the world for a witness unto all nations. What proportion of the ten thousand or fifty thousand patients treated in a hospital in one year embrace Christianity? The best definition for a chapel is a hospital for sin-sick souls. Many an humble preacher when asked, "Where are your converts?" can reply, "These are they which . . . have washed their robes, and made them white in the blood of the Lamb. Therefore are they before the throne of God." Of some laborious missionaries it may be said, "These all died in faith, not having received the promises, but having seen them afar off, and were persuaded of them and embraced them." How full of tenderness are the simple words of the writer to the Hebrews, "For God is not unrighteous to forget your work and labor of love."

CHAPTER V.

Itineration and Woman's Work.

THOUGH the prophets of the Old Testament economy travelled much of their time as Samuel, who "went from year to year in circuit" to hold court; or as Elijah and Elisha, who taught the people in the city and in the forest, and spake, "Thus saith the Lord" to kings and priests; or as Isaiah, who "walked naked and barefoot" three years throughout the coasts of Israel, yet the true itinerancy began with our Lord in Judea, and was carried on throughout the known world by the twelve apostles of the Lamb. "These twelve Jesus sent forth, and commanded them, saying, Go, . . . And as ye go, preach." "After these things the Lord appointed other seventy also, and sent them two and two before his face into every city and place whither he himself would come." His instructions were, to go *before his face*, and to go *into every city and place whither he himself would come*. And when the disciples returned they came unto "Jesus and told him all things, both what they had done and what they had taught." This is an example that each tour must be ended by a report to the Master.

In China, missionary circuits are of three kinds. The first, the city and its suburbs; the second, the county or the prefecture; the third, a wide extent of country with its mighty cities and flourishing towns. The man of God is not to confine his labors to the chapel; he must also be a pedestrian preacher, and gain the advantage of both the outdoor and indoor methods. Along the streets he may reach numbers, and have groups of from ten to thirty to listen for fifteen or twenty minutes. Thus short sermons preached in a forenoon in several different localities will be heard by many persons; or by tract-distribution from house to house, speaking a word to each one, the living preacher may bear witness for Christ. It is important for the missionary to go once a day to some busy mart, and there preach regularly. In the courts of the temples, the open spaces of the city, at the gates, and upon the highways—wherever men are to be found—the servants of the King are to compel them to come in unto the wedding supper. The Spirit of the Lord may touch a heart, and lead some one to the chapel to receive instruction.

The second circuit is that of the county or the prefecture, a field of labor within definite bounds, is the region of country which the central chapel directly influences. By itinerating in this section, the city and country work mutually act and react on each other. The peasant coming to town recognizes the missionary as an acquaintance, and feels as if he meets a friend in a strange city. It is important "to ride this circuit" several times a year, regularly, patiently, painstakingly, and so continue in well-doing till the seed springs up and bears fruit. When groups of native churches are established, these demand much of the itinerant's attention and care, that they may become both self-sustaining and self-supporting. The minister grows weary in town, and the hills and dales, so densely populated, furnish recreating labor. The Master spent much of his time in the villages. The tea-shop, with fifty or a hundred men sipping the national beverage, may be converted into a chapel by the purchase of a cup of tea, and all listen for a few minutes. In the open spaces of the towns, a congregation—from twenty to five hundred—will assemble, and listen to something they have not heard before. In the hamlets, a bench is brought out, a cup of tea offered, a number sit around, the preacher is asked to talk, and the children ordered to be silent. There is nothing more striking than the courtesy of the farmers and the kindness they show to a foreigner. Passing through the fields, and talking to the country people, a number will propose to take a smoke, and, seated on the green turf, will converse for a half-hour on gospel themes. One of the most effective modes of work is by regular appointments for preaching at night, when the neighbors, the labors of the day finished, will assemble, and remain till the service is ended. The opportunities in the country for a minister to preach to the women are unbounded; in fact, the large majority of the listeners belong to the gentler sex.

While there remains such a vast amount of unoccupied territory, missionaries must occasionally take long evangelistic tours, covering a vast extent of country. One of the most effective methods, when only one or two days can be given to a place, is colportage. Where several hundred books, tracts, and portions of the Bible can be sold in one day, it seems wise to leave the written word in the place. It is only those who have travelled through the land who can appreciate the excitement which the presence of a foreigner creates. When the enthusiasm is so keenly aroused, a fine opportunity is afforded to make known the primary truths of Christianity. In the South, the mode of travel is by boats, which become a temporary residence. In the North, where they travel in carts, on wheelbarrows, or on donkeys, they stop in the inns, and these at times become Bethels. The soft spring days and the beautiful autumns invite the gospel farmer to go out into the country, and through this instrumentality many thousands have been brought into the kingdom. The Chinese peasant prepares a plat, pumping on water, and working up to the knees in mud, till not a lump remains, and it is of the consistency of thin syrup; then he walks along the bank and broadcasts the grain, which springs up a beautiful carpet of green, and these sprouts are transplanted into the fields. "Cast thy bread upon the waters; for thou shalt find it after many days."

In the short discourse at Jacob's well, which Jesus delivered to his disciples, he bids them not to tarry: "Say not ye, There are yet four months, and then cometh harvest? Behold, I say unto you, Lift up your eyes, and look on the fields; for they are white already to harvest." Our Master would not say to those preaching in China, "I sent you to reap that whereon ye bestowed no labor; other men labored, and ye are entered into their labors"; for no prophets have gone before us exhorting the people to worship Jehovah. The Saviour tells us that one laborer follows another.

He says: "And herein is that saying true, One soweth, and another reapeth." One of the keenest joys known to the minister is the gathering in of converts, but there is as much joy in sowing as in reaping, "that both he that soweth and he that reapeth may rejoice together."

Woman's Work for Women.

The hearts of godly women have been turned to their benighted sisters in pagan lands, and help has been sent. The object is not to bring future generations to the knowledge of the truth, but to labor for the salvation of those who now live and move,—our contemporaries. It is a beautiful inscription upon the flag the ladies fly at the masthead, "Woman's Work for Women"; not "Woman's Work for Girls," but what is technically called "The Zenana Work," or talking to adult females about Christ and his redemption. When we consider the influence of a heathen mother and the efforts she puts forth to teach her children idolatry, we realize the transcendent importance of this department of labor. When mothers are brought to Christ, then we may hope for the conversion of the children and the establishment of a church. The work in the cities in China is conducted by visiting from house to house, receiving visitors in the "Home," forming voluntary classes for religious instruction, and by the Sabbath afternoon meetings for women. As the lady passes along the more retired streets, how many invitations to come in, and how many esteem it a privilege to have a foreign visitor! Some have been more successful in connecting the medical work with the spiritual, and ministering to the sick in their houses, and whenever a dose of medicine was given at the foreigner's residence, to follow it up by a visit at the native's home. It is wonderful what an influence in a large field a lady in active work may thus gain in a few years. Her name a household word, her presence greeted with a smile, her counsels listened to with pleasure, her inquiries after the sick, the aged and the young, answered with respect, her labors become the ideal of pastoral work, and she is received by the people as a ministering angel.

The difficulties of laboring at the ports are greater than in the interior, so it is quite desirable for the ladies to be located in the inland towns and villages, where they have free access to the multitudes. In all central China, and in many other sections of the empire, a lady may itinerate with perfect freedom, travel from village to village, and visit from hamlet to hamlet. Working in a definite field is, perhaps, more effective.

How direct the work when the gospel is presented to them one by one, or a group eagerly listening to the first message; when the heavy mists of superstition are rolled away, and the consolations of religion are offered to them in their sorrow! The appeals are so pointed, the opportunities to divert the conversation into spiritual channels so multiform, the receptions in the parlor so homelike, the atmosphere of the woman's meeting so genial and sympathetic, such a nearness and mutual attraction, that these become precious seasons when the dews of gospel grace are gently distilled. Instead of a few hundred, we long for a host of holy women, who will seek the millions wandering upon the mountains of idolatry, and, like good shepherdesses, bring them to the fold of Christ. The Chinese have a proverb, "Good men and believing women," which shows that here, as throughout the world, woman's heart is more susceptible of religious impressions than man's; and, as this is a most delightful form of evangelistic labor, the room where the women meet often becomes like unto the Mount of Transfiguration. The one who tells the "old, old story," is surprised to find "that the springs which awaken religious thought are so easily touched; that an unseen hand has gone before, and has already swept over those chords and set them vibrating, which, in the renewed heart, produce immortal harmonies, like those in the hearts of our first parents in Eden." The Psalmist says, "The Lord giveth the word: the women that publish the tidings are a great host." (*Revised Version.*) May there come to this land "a great host" of godly women, who will publish to those of their own sex "the tidings," teaching the adult women of China the word of the Lord!

CHAPTER VI.

The Spiritual Kingdom.

IT is common to speak of the various means used for Christianizing the heathen as so many *branches* of missionary labor, and to place them side by side as of equal importance. There is scarcely a phrase more likely to mislead than the term "missionary work," as if it consisted of several departments of evangelistic labor. The press, the school, the hospital, and the chapel are considered the four pillars of a great edifice which the people of God are erecting on a heathen shore. This view is incorrect. Preaching is THE TEMPLE, and tracts, medicine, and education are as the houses for the priests, the chambers built round about, and the outer courts of the sacred place. Preaching is the sum and substance of missionary work. Other forms of labor are admissible, but they are simply auxiliaries. They are secondary, and not primary; assistants, and not the principal; supplementary, and not the chief work. The auxiliaries are worthy of all honor, if, *first*, in comparison with preaching, the sun of missions, they are small planets; and *second*, that they revolve around the sun, and do not, like comets, fly off at a tangent. What if Paul had had a mission press to issue his letters by the million? Would he not have used this mighty engine of modern civilization? There is no land where labor and paper is as cheap, so that the printed page is an effective method of evangelization. Tracts are issued by hundreds of thousands, and point out the way of life to all who read. And is not the command of our Lord, "Heal the sick"? Were not those three happy years for Judea when "Jesus went about all the cities and villages, ... healing every sickness and every disease among the people"? Does not the medical work represent Christianity in its most attractive features to pagan nations? And is there not a direct connection between healing the poor, sick body and the sin-sick soul? As a matter of fact, the hospital is in a measure a combination of the church and the street chapel. There is daily preaching at the dispensary, and regular services in the wards. Medical men like the late Kenneth Mackenzie make a profound spiritual impression upon the tens of thousands whose diseases they heal.

The press, the hospital, and the school are the three fair handmaidens attending the ministry, but the greatest of these is the school. The resurrected Jesus, in his brief, but touching, discourse at the "seaside" breakfast-table, said that the proof of love was, "Feed my lambs." Surely the little multitude, which at evening time throng every street, are not to be left alone, with no effort to do them good. Surrounded as they are by heathen influences, the Sunday-school is not enough to stem the current of idolatry and superstition, but they must be gathered into "seven-days Sabbath-schools," which is the best definition of the Bible-taught day-schools. Passing upwards, the college, or school of high grade, is a necessity; for the apostle, in speaking of the ministry, enjoined: "The same commit thou to faithful men who shall be able to teach others also." A command embraces all that is necessary for its execution. It is a reasonable hope, that from a number of thoroughly trained men, God shall call to the ministry some who are "apt to teach." The curriculum of the native schools furnishes not one element of practical knowledge, and, in addition, they are idolatrous. The churches must look, in a large measure, to the mission schools for their pastors. It is most desirable that the societies should send out a corps of professional teachers, laymen, who are called to teach, but not to preach, and who can devote themselves wholly to the one work.

As to the diaconate, the apostles could say: "It is not reason that we should leave the word of God to serve tables. Wherefore, brethren, look ye out from among you . . . men . . whom we may appoint over this business." And why? "We will give ourselves continually to prayer and to the ministry of the word," the two greatest things known in the church. Yet, from the ministerial ranks in every nation rise distinguished educators, who exercise a mighty influence upon morality and religion It is also very difficult to obtain teachers. Many men can preach, but only a few combine the literary and executive ability necessary to conduct a school. In the mission field, these may be considered the most useful of men, for they gather into their institutions of learning the children of the converts of many missionaries, train the pastors and teachers for the rising churches, and thus have much direct fruit from their labors. But, while this is true, education must occupy a subordinate position in the world's evangelization; it must only be an incidental part of the scheme. There must be a "proportion of faith." If the main body of evangelists—by far the vast majority—give their time wholly to "holding forth the word of life," then we may confidently expect that the spiritual kingdom of the Redeemer will be established.

Except in a few instances, it cannot be said that undue attention is paid to education in this land at the present time. China sleeps, and it is almost as hard to get the scholars to learn geography as to study the Bible, but when she awakes and the cry comes on every side, "Teach me!" "Teach me!" there is danger that the church will turn aside from her main calling. It is the case in Japan, where only one-third of the ministerial force is engaged in preaching. They have listened to the siren voice of the native press calling them from the pulpit to the professional chair. In India, we learn that some whole missions give all their energy to reaching the brain instead of the heart. There are breakers ahead, and the China church should awake to the danger!

The duty of the disciple is simply to obey the parting instructions of his departing Lord, "Go, go; go ye, go ye out, out into all the world and preach the gospel to every creature." The Duke of Wellington said, "Let the church obey her marching orders." Paul said to Agrippa, "I was not disobedient, O king, unto the heavenly vision." A month before the surrender at Appomattox, in the third watch of the night, General Lee summoned Lieutenant-General Gordon to his headquarters, and, leaning upon the mantle, told him sadly that his army was 46,000 against 160,000; that his supplies were cut off, and sure defeat awaited them. "Go, then," said his Lieutenant, "to Richmond, and urge Congress to make peace on the best terms it can get." General Lee raised himself erect and said, "General Gordon, I am a soldier." May not the preacher sometimes feel that legislative functions pertain to his office, and forget that he is simply a soldier? Senator Evarts, the son of the great Missionary Secretary, is credited with saying, " Brethren of the ministry, stick to your calling; preach the word; make full proof of your ministry." The distinction must be clearly made between a philanthropist and a minister. The one aims to do good, the other, to preach the gospel; the one, to instruct; the other, to regenerate; the one, what is useful; the other, what is essential to salvation. Every active Christian may lead an intensely useful life in China and do a great deal of good, but the church's strength must not be frittered away in its benevolent departments, whether relating to the mind or the body. In this land missionary work may be defined, "The time spent in imparting religious truth to the Chinese."

The Saviour says, "My kingdom is not of this world." It is a spiritual kingdom, where, under the guidance of the Holy Spirit, men worship Jehovah, who is a Spirit, in spirit and in truth. The term "spiritual kingdom" is commonly used in juxtaposition to "political kingdom," but is equally the opposite of an educational kingdom, though the school is an essential accompaniment of the church. If education is apparently the chief aim, as the Chinese have no true conception of the body of Christ, may they not mistake the school with its sciences for the church where the Bible is taught? As Rev. Griffeth John said, May 10, 1877, "We are here not to develop the resources of the country, not for the advancement of commerce, not for the mere promotion of civilization, but to do battle with the powers of darkness, to save men from sin and conquer China for Christ. Commerce and science are good in their place. We do not underrate their importance. They might develop in China a new and higher form of civilization,—a civilization that would bring with it abundant wealth, rich stores of knowledge, and many contrivances to lighten the burden of existence, and make life more happy than it is, but they cannot meet a single spiritual want, still a single spiritual craving, or infuse the life of God into a single soul. The gospel alone is the power of God unto salvation; and salvation from the guilt and dominion of sin—from moral and spiritual misery—is the great need of the Chinese. Believing this, we devote ourselves to the supreme work of making known to them the truth as it is in Jesus, as far as we can, and of commending it to their hearts and consciences in every possible way."

We come as spiritual men, taught by the Holy Spirit, filled with the Holy Spirit, sent by the Holy Spirit, to minister in holy things. It is not enough that we be spiritually minded, we must labor in a spiritual calling; not enough that our affections be set on things above, our voices must speak spiritual truths. In the holy war, spiritual weapons are to be used. Paul says, "For the weapons of our warfare are not carnal, but mighty, through God, to the pulling down of strongholds." Geography, arithmetic, astronomy, history, chemistry, are not spiritual weapons, and, though they are good in their proper sphere, they are not mighty to demolish Satan's kingdom. Our direct work is not to reform the Chinese system of education, for in it there is much that is excellent, but to overthrow their religious systems, which are abominations. It is important to lead the mind into the broad fields of knowledge, but much more important to guide souls into the happier fields of Eden. In the touching parody, *A Missionary Teacher's Lament*, occurs this couplet (italics ours):

> "Eight clever native boys, *being taught of heaven*,
> By *study of geography* are soon reduced to seven."

The missionary preacher often laments his apparent want of success, but in teaching about heaven he uses The Revelation as his text-book.

Our Lord says: "For which of you, intending to build a tower, sitteth not down first, and counteth the cost?" The Head of the church has commanded his disciples to preach the gospel to this nation; and, as he is omnipotent and omniscient, we have faith that, if the church will perform her duty, the work will be accomplished by divine power. If, however, we attempt the gigantic task of educating four hundred millions, are we assured that some may not "begin to mock, and say, This man began to build, and was not able to finish"? Is it right for the church to attempt the double Herculean task of christianizing and educating? Let the school be used only as a means for conserving the interests of the kingdom. The heralds upon the walls of Zion must not mistake *material progress* for the coming of the kingdom of righteousness, neither are they to look for a harvest, save as the seed is the word of God. The apostle says: "Be not deceived; God is not mocked: for whatsoever a man soweth, that shall he also reap. For he that soweth to his flesh shall of the flesh reap corruption; but he that soweth to the Spirit shall of the Spirit reap life everlasting. And let us not be weary in well-doing; for in due season we shall reap, if we faint not." The law of harvests is universal. We cannot expect a religious crop from scientific planting. The first preacher to the Gentiles summed up his work of husbandry in Corinth: "We have sown unto you spiritual things." We rejoice in the introduction of railways, telegraphs, steamships, scientific apparatus, and all of which a European civilization boasts; and if the gospel be vigorously preached, these may prove aids to the introduction of Christianity; but, on the contrary, should the people accept civilization and reject Christianity, it may be said: "If the light that is in thee be darkness, how great is that darkness!"

There is no lack of examples of the course to be pursued. The designation of the prophets was "men of God." Their summons was, "Hear ye the word of the Lord." And is the glory of the ministry under this dispensation less than that of the old? The apostles preached Jesus and the resurrection. In his address to the presbytery at Ephesus, Paul said: "So that I might finish my course with joy, and the ministry which I have received of the Lord Jesus, to testify the gospel of the grace of God. And now, behold, I know that ye all, among whom I have gone preaching the kingdom of God, shall see my face no more. Wherefore I take you to record this day, that I am pure from the blood of all men. For I have not shunned to declare unto you all the counsel of God." We are ordered to "teach all nations," but Christ limited the text-books to sixty-six—"teaching them to observe all things whatsoever I command you." We are not to accept Beecher's definition of preaching "Christ and him crucified" as including "geography, history, science, or whatever would elevate and benefit mankind." It is only the Scriptures that are inspired.

It is sometimes said that the great object of the missionary is to train men for the ministry. This is putting a part for the whole. A native ministry is the ripe fruit of the rising church, and not the original seed. Suppose all the doctors should spend their whole time in training native physicians; where, then, would be the sick, the lame, and the blind? And shall the physicians of souls say their mission is of less importance than that of the medical profession?

In the evangelization of benighted nations it is important that the societies, boards, and committees be composed of men who not only have a zeal for God's glory, but who also have experienced the joys of a call to preach. As ministers' wives have always been intimately connected with the preaching of the cross, perhaps they are best fitted for serving on ladies' boards and sending out holy women, who will enter "the great door" which is opened to them of visiting from house to house and bringing mothers to Jesus. First win the mothers, and the sons will, like Timothy, be "wise unto salvation." The object of Woman's Work for Women is not female education, but their salvation.

The work among the heathen demands men who, like Paul, can say, "Yea, woe is me if I preach not the gospel." The two mottoes are, "Knowing, therefore, the terror of the Lord, we persuade men"; and, "The love of Christ constraineth us." Jeremiah gives his experience: "Then I said, I will not make mention of him, nor speak any more in his name. But his word was in mine heart as a burning fire shut up in my bones, and I was weary with forbearing and I could not stay;" therefore, he did not continue a *silenced* preacher. Missionary work also demands men of strong faith, not only faith in God, but faith in preaching as the power of God unto salvation. He must put aside "the *evil* heart of unbelief" and believe that the spoken word will not "return void." This preaching on naked faith, with few converts, tries the husbandman who has need of long patience. It is not pleasant to walk along the streets of an idolatrous city, amidst the darkness of superstition, and "perpetually encounter the pride, indifference, hypocrisy, absurdities, stolid ignorance, and inveterate prejudice" with which we meet, and so we need foreheads "as an adamant harder than flint."

The apostle tells us of the certainties of the gospel, "We having the same spirit of faith, according as it is written, I believed, and therefore have I spoken; we also believe, and therefore speak." If preaching is not the way by which the world is to be converted, then we must conclude that the risen Saviour made a mistake. Is the Lord's hand shortened that it cannot save by preaching, and must it be lengthened by ways and means of man's devising? Says Christ, "If a man walk in the day," *i. e.*, in the path of duty, "he stumbleth not." Look at the preaching history of Methodism and its giant growth, and shall not the methods so successful in the Occident work well in the Orient?

We are to rejoice in every effort for the advancement of the church of the living God. Let the press issue her books and tracts by the million, let the schools educate their thousands, and the hospitals their ten thousands, but, above all, let the pulpit maintain its prestige. Two *per cent.* of the missionary body is quite enough for all agencies. The number of physicians who exercise their divine gift of healing will not likely exceed ten *per cent.*, and if one in ten of the whole force is engaged in teaching it is sufficient to conserve the interests of Zion and to promote those of science. What would the evangelist do without Bibles and tracts for colportage, which is the help-meet of oral preaching? Without the physician to care for the sick, the missionary ranks would be rapidly reduced, and besides, how blessed to see the balm of Gilead administered to the sick, to behold the lame man leaping as an hart, and sight restored to the blind! The ministry owe to laborious educators a debt of gratitude for the efficient aid they render in preparing native preachers and teachers for their assistants. Deducting those engaged in the academy and the hospital, there will be three-fourths of the missionaries left for spiritual work. We are sure this is not an extreme view. Fidelity to our Lord demands that we claim that the large majority of those who are sent shall minister at the altar, and be ever ready to preach the gospel. When men, like the late Norman McLeod, returning from a tour of missionary inspection in India, advocate the educational policy, or, like the sainted Alexander Duff, who said, "Let me reach the brain," we take issue and cry, Time to teach, when Christ says preach! time to teach, when the Macedonian cry is heard! time to teach, when the pestilence is raging! time to teach, when men are perishing for the bread of life! time to teach, when death is near! time to teach, when eternity is at hand! We are to beware of taking the broad view of missionary work, for it is like walking in the broad road; the narrow way of Christ's commands is the safest. There is need of caution from all, lest the river, clear as crystal, which flows from underneath the throne, so graphically described as deepening and widening and bringing life and healing to the nations, be like the Yellow River, "China's sorrow," which, diverted from its natural course, finds its way to the sea by a channel too narrow, and proves so disastrious to Shantoong and Honan. When there was no eye to pity and no arm to save, then stepped forth the Son of God and cried, "I delight to do thy will, O my God; yea, thy law is within my heart. I have preached righteousness in the great congregation; lo, I have not refrained my lips, O Lord, thou knowest."

CHAPTER VII.

THE AMBASSADOR TO SINIM.

IN a land of schools and scholars, it is hard to imagine the prestige of a western teacher in the Middle Kingdom. With the advantage of being accepted as a scholar, how ought the minister of the New Testament to endeavor to show forth the higher life of a disciple of Christ! The ideal teacher of the Chinese is a holy man: "He is entirely sincere, and perfect in love. He is magnanimous, generous, benign, and full of forbearance. He is pure in heart, free from selfishness, and never swerves from the path of duty in his conduct. He is deep and active, like a fountain, sending forth his virtues in due season. He is seen, and men revere him; he speaks, and men believe him; he acts, and men are gladdened by him. He possesses all heavenly virtues. He is one with heaven." Since the Bible unites religion and morality, how much is required of the missionary in manifesting Jehoveh's name unto those to whom he is sent! They know not God, but they study him as revealed by his servants. They have not the Bible, but they read the lives and characters of those who profess to be guided by its truths. If one asks, "Who is sufficient for these things?" it may be answered: "Like as a father pitieth his children, so the Lord pitieth them that fear him. For he knoweth our frame; he remembereth that we are dust."

It is of prime importance that the evangelist be a holy man. Are not all the disciples called *saints?* "Ye are witnesses, and God also, how holily and justly and unblamably we behaved ourselves among you," said Paul, in his letter to Thessalonica. The minister "must be blameless," "That ye may be blameless and harmless, the sons of God, without rebuke, in the midst of a crooked and perverse nation, among whom ye shine as lights in the world." The qualifications for the teaching elder, given in the pastoral epistles, refer mostly to the moral character, and very briefly to intellectual endowments. It is not required that the man of God profess holiness, but it is demanded that he cultivate personal piety.

The minister to the Chinese must be a prayerful man. There will be moments on the mount when, like Moses, he holds communion with God. "If I have grace in thy sight, show me now thy way." "And he said, My presence shall go with thee, and I will give thee rest." "I beseech thee, show me thy glory." "And he said, I will make all my goodness pass before thee." Did not the Great Missionary, after busy days of preaching and healing, spend whole nights in communion with his Father, in order to obtain spiritual strength for the work of the morrow? The apostle to the Gentiles magnified his office in that he prayed for his converts from heathenism. "Without ceasing I make mention of you in my prayers." I "do not cease to pray for you, and to desire that ye be filled with knowledge of his will in all wisdom and spiritual understanding, that ye might walk worthy of the Lord unto all pleasing, being faithful in every good work, and increasing in the knowledge of God; strengthened with all might, according to his glorious power, unto all patience and long-suffering with joyfulness." I "cease not to give thanks for you, making mention of you in my prayers; that the God of our Lord Jesus Christ, the Father of glory, may give unto you the spirit of wisdom and revelation in the knowledge of him: the eyes of your understanding being enlightened; that ye may know what is the hope of his calling, and what the riches of the glory of his inheritance in the saints, and what is the exceeding greatness of his power to us-ward who believe, according to the working of his mighty power." "For this cause I bow my knees unto the Father of our Lord Jesus Christ, of whom the whole family in heaven and earth is named, that he would grant you, according to the riches of his glory, to be strengthened with might by his Spirit in the inner man: that Christ may dwell in your hearts by faith; that ye, being rooted and grounded in love, may be able to comprehend, with all saints, what is the breadth, and length, and depth, and height: and to know the love of Christ, which passeth knowledge; that ye may be filled with all the fulness of God."

Faith is also a prime requisite in him that lays the foundations of the future church. He must have faith in God, faith in the Bible as the word of God, faith in preaching as the appointed instrument for the conversion of men, faith in the men who are converted, faith in the millennium promises, faith in Christ as the King and Head of the church. He walks by faith, and lives by faith. His motto is: "The life which I now live in the flesh, I live by the faith of the Son of God."

The missionary's vital energy comes from the Holy Spirit. Paul forcibly puts it: "Be not drunk with wine, wherein is excess; but be filled with the Spirit," wherein there can be no excess. The "beloved physician" quotes his Master when he declares: "But ye shall receive power, after that the Holy Ghost is come upon you," and ye shall "be endued with power from on high." Not power in this age to work miracles, or to convert men, but a power to be "in the Spirit on the Lord's day," a power to speak earnestly, a power to arrest the attention of the audience, a power to be like a hot stove, sending out heat to every quarter; a power to convince men that we speak the experience of our own hearts. The preacher, in all ages of the church, has had power over vast assemblies, for there is a magnetism in intellectual and spiritual gifts. Stephen is described as a man "full of faith and power." As a man of power, the Bible places before all laborers who contend against idolatry, the giant character of Elijah. Of the forerunner of the Messiah the prophetic description was given: "And he shall go before him in the spirit and power of Elias." Though the extraordinary gifts possessed by the early church may not be ours, yet the ordinary gifts are bestowed upon the disciples abundantly at this time.

The herald of the cross must be entirely consecrated to the work. The apostle gives us a chapter on consecration: "But what things were gain to me, those I counted loss for Christ. Yea, doubtless, and I count all things but loss for the excellency of the knowledge of Christ Jesus my Lord; for whom I have suffered the loss of all things, and do count them but dung, that I may win Christ, and be found in him, not having mine own righteousness, which is of the law, but that which is through the faith of Christ, the righteousness which is of God by faith; that I may know him, and the power of his resurrection, and the fellowship of his sufferings, being made conformable unto his death; if by any means I might attain unto the resurrection of the dead. Not as though I had already attained, either were already perfect; but I follow after, if that I may apprehend that for which I am apprehended of Christ Jesus. Brethren, I count not myself to have apprehended; but this one thing I do, forgetting those things which are behind, and reaching forth unto those things which are before, I press toward the mark for the prize of the high calling of God in Christ Jesus."

He must also be "all things to all men." The apostle stated his object in this ready adaptability to the varied conditions of the peoples to whom he ministered: "I am made all things to all men, that I might by all means save some." We do not suppose that he specially referred to man *millinery*, or man *commissary*, or man *ceremony*, but to the higher and more important affairs of the mind and heart. He was a true minister, and, as "the Son of man came not to be ministered unto, but to minister," so Paul said, "I made myself servant unto all, that I might gain the more." With the Jews, he drew his arguments from the Old Testament Scriptures; preaching to the Gentiles, he appealed to conscience. For fear of offending the weak brethren, he ate not the food which had been offered to idols or ancestors. If salary caused his parishioners to say that he "ate the church's rice," he labored at his old trade, though he taught that the Lord ordained that the preacher "should live of the gospel." In his intercourse with men he sought for that which is expedient, appropriate, and seasonable. Those who follow the apostle in his missionary journeys should study the deep spiritual meaning of his words when he says, "This I do for the gospel's sake."

The missionary must lead a life of *self-denial*. It is not enough that "he go out, not knowing whither he goeth," but that he ever keep his body in subjection. Among a people where existence is reduced to the minimum, his style of living should be as simple as is conducive to health and comfort, for at the lowest it seems extravagant to the Chinese. On the other hand, he should avoid asceticism in all its forms. The Master associated with all classes, and though he had not where to lay his head, yet he joyfully accepted the invitations to the feasts prepared in his honor. There is a happy medium, which is left to the good sense of each laborer.

Joy is one of the highest requisites in the catagory of missionary graces. Amidst difficulties, foes without and dissensions within, Nehemiah said to the returned captives at Jerusalem, "The joy of the Lord is your strength." The minister is to "rejoice evermore." Day by day his spirits must soar upwards as the lark. There is nothing more dangerous than depression. A man cannot bear the burden of idolatry of a great nation. He is simply to stand in his appointed place and testify against it. He is daily to give thanks that among the Gentiles he may declare the unsearchable riches of Christ. He is to rejoice in his converts, and, like Paul, to ask, "For what is our hope, or joy, or crown of rejoicing?" and himself give the answer, "Ye are our glory and joy." He is to keep his eye fixed on the future rewards of the faithful watchman. He is to rejoice with joy unspeakable, and be glad with exceeding joy. "A merry heart maketh a cheerful countenance." "A merry heart doeth good like a medicine." The pressure of study and work is too great for any one to sustain without the spring and buoyant influence of a hearty laugh. What incentives to joy? The Saviour commanding, the church sending, prayers ascending, heaven awaiting, is this not joy?

Paul gives the advice to Timothy, and, through him, to all who labor in distant lands, "Take heed unto thyself." Not to watch simply the methods and ways of work, or his diligence in performing his duty, but to look well to his own personal condition. Away from home, amidst heathen influences, and with Christians recently reclaimed from paganism, there is need to "watch and pray." Each one must say, "I keep under my body, and bring it into subjection, lest that by any means, when I preach to others, I myself should be a castaway."

Above all, he needs to possess a sympathetic heart. He must be a Chinese of the Chinese, and feel for the people in their poverty, ignorance, superstition, and idolatry; "Who can have compassion on the ignorant, and on them that are out of the way, for that he himself also is compassed with infirmity." "For we have not an high priest who cannot be touched with the feeling of our infirmities." And this sympathy must ripen into love.

Love to the sheep is a mark of the true Shepherd, who, "having loved his own, loved them unto the end." No one is prepared for work among any race without a love to the people. How the epistles abound in testimonies of the ardent love of the pastor for the flock! Hundreds of missionaries in Sinim can exclaim: "Oh, ye Chinese, our mouth is open unto you, our heart is enlarged. Ye are not straitened in us, but ye are straitened in your own bowels."

The crowning gift of the preacher is humility. King David never forgot that God "took him from the sheep-cote, ... and brought him to feed Jacob, his people; and Israel, his inheritance." Paul said, "For I am the least of the apostles, that am not meet to be called an apostle," and termed himself "the least of all saints," yea, "the chief of sinners." No shadow of egotism must be suffered to darken the heart or life of the laborer—"my church," "my work," "my converts." Day by day God's name is to be praised. "Not unto us, not unto us, but unto thy name be the glory." In one word, the spiritual life of the disciple must be summed up in the invitation of Christ: "Learn of me, for I am meek and lowly in heart, and ye shall find rest for your souls."

CHAPTER VIII.

Literary Preparation.

WHEN the apostles were sent forth to establish a new religion, prominent among their endowments was the "gift of tongues." At the descent of the Holy Ghost at Pentecost, "There appeared unto them cloven tongues as of fire, and it sat upon each of them, . . . and they began to speak with other tongues. . . . The multitude came together, and were confounded, because that every man heard them speak in his own language." Thus was ability given them to go from land to land proclaiming the gospel. The great apostle could say, "I spake with more tongues than ye all";—he was the most distinguished linguist the world has ever seen. This miraculous gift of tongues must have produced a wonderful impression upon the nations of the earth, and attested the divine origin of the religion the first preachers came to establish. This heaven-bestowed endowment of being able in a moment to speak in a foreign language has ceased, but we have no doubt that, in answer to prayer, the gift of tongues is still bestowed upon those who diligently use the means placed at their disposal.

The language-student has many advantages: first and foremost, a dictionary of surpassing merit in its perspicuity, and also the numerous primers, vocabularies, and hand-books. He has, too, the blessing of possessing a teacher who does not know a word of English, for with an English-speaking preceptor the task is almost hopeless. During the first years the novice is in a most trying position. He graduates at college, takes a three-years course in a theological hall, is ordained as an ambassador to the heathen, and, landing upon a distant shore, finds himself as helpless as an infant, without the infant's privilege of making its wants known by crying. A royal road to the acquisition of the Chinese language has not yet been discovered. There is not the slightest connection between this tongue and European languages, and former studies into Latin and Greek roots afford no aid. Also it is one thing to learn to read a dead language, and quite another to be able to speak a living tongue. The young missionary's whole time and energy should be devoted to the arduous task. Till his lips are unsealed, and he can speak with the tongues of men, he is simply an incubus upon the society that supports him. Were he at home, he could employ his time in preaching, and thus try to do some good, but now his lips are sealed. Surely he should make every effort to shorten his probation. As Paul says, "I had rather speak five words with my understanding"; and again, "Therefore, if I know not the meaning of the voice, I shall be unto him that speaketh a barbarian." Much responsibility rests upon the seniors in the field in pressing upon the new arrival the absolute necessity of constant and earnest effort to learn to talk, and at first giving them daily some aid. The young missionary with an earnest desire to engage in work as soon as he arrives upon the field, may imagine that he can be useful by teaching English while he is at the rudiments of the language. The policy of English and Chinese, half-and-half, is suicidal in respect to one's future ministry. If English is desirable, it should be taught either by those who have learned the language, or by those who never expect to study it. By six hours a day devoted to study, and constant association with the people, any man of rather more than ordinary ability may in three years learn to speak Chinese moderately well. If, then, he teaches English three hours, how long will it take him? It may be answered that this is a simple sum in arithmetic. If, however, we appeal to mathematics, there is the problem of the snail which crawled up the post four feet during the day, and slipped back two feet at night. If he studies Chinese in the forenoon, and teaches English in the afternoon, his progress will be that of the snail. The Chinese language is too intricate and too difficult to allow of half-way measures. The man must learn to think before he is able to speak, and English must be banished by the expulsive power of a new tongue. When one sees a Chinaman, he must think in Chinese, if he desires to speak with ease. Besides putting off the day of preaching indefinitely, the semi-student will likely become discouraged, and remit his sturdy efforts. Among the China missionaries good speakers are the rule, and only now and then do we meet with an exception; but in the Sunrise Kingdom, where they talk with English-speaking Japanese, and teach English daily, many may truly say, "I spake as a child." The church allows three years to the student-missionary to prepare for life's warfare. Let him, as "a good soldier of Jesus Christ," not "entangle himself with the affairs of this life; that he may please him who hath chosen him to be a soldier."

It is necessary for the preacher to the heathen to *speak fluently*. We must preach so as to com-mend the gospel to the favorable consideration of the people. As long as the audience is busy noting grammatical errors, we can make little progress in instilling religious truth. No one need say, "I have no gift of language." Let the young brother become as a little child, and prattle everything he hears, not waiting to comprehend the meaning. Let him study for hours in his office, and then daily throw himself among the people—in the tea-shops, along the market-places, at the coolie-stands, on the bridges—in his notebook carefully jotting down every new expression, or with his teacher along the streets, studying the language as it is written on the hanging signs, and soon he will find himself swimming in a sea of words. The streets are full of boys and men who are ready to teach, and who charge no fee; they are pedagogues just for the fun. There are two great books, the book of written characters and the book of living voices. These are the two sides of the linguistic arch. If the student pursues the indoor method, his Chinese will sound to the ear just as Wickliffe's Version appears to the eye; if, on the other hand, he neglects his text-books, his vocabulary will be superficial; but if he learns a sentence within, and tries to use it on the street, the people ere long will say, "Why, you talk just like we do." We are not to daub the walls of Zion with mud, but, like Solomon, to "build of stone made ready before it was brought thither." If we speak to the people "with stammering lips and another tongue," and our own countrymen would not listen to us in a land where Christianity is accepted, how can we expect to impress those who do not believe in our religion? Just as a little urchin was asked, "What are you going to be?" "Going to be a preacher." "Where are you going to preach?" "In China." "Well, *what* are you going to preach in China?" "I am going to preach *Chinese*." This was not the answer desired, but it illustrates the point: a preacher in China must preach Chinese. We must aim at a high standard in the vernacular. A sinologue is one who is a master in Chinese lore, but a colloquial scholarship is of a much higher order than classical learning, just as to preach a sermon requires more skill than to write one. Each one must bring his gifts to the altar. Missionary life does not consist wholly in prayers and holy living, for a ready tongue is a prime factor.

We come to a land rich in its mines of language. There is nothing in the literature of China but language. Nothing is taught in the schools but language—merely the department of *belle-lettres* or English literature in our colleges—and a diploma is granted to the elect few who can write pretty essays; so the verbiage of China, like tropical foliage, is precociously developed. There is a wealth of idiom, a variety of synonym, a diversity of expression, an infinity of phraseology, that gives every possible shade of meaning, and opens a wide-extended field for the speaker. The materials for oratory are all here, and the earth opens her stores to those who seek for hid treasure. Let all the studies bend to the one object of being a workman who needeth not to be ashamed in the pulpit. There is a very practical thought: A home congregation will, out of respect for the sanctuary, remain seated till the benediction is pronounced; but here a man must enchain his audience by the mode of presenting the truth. To preach to the native Christians is easy, as we have only to expound the Bible, which they receive as a revelation from God; but when we come to men who accept nothing, believe nothing, and hope for nothing, and when the only basis of our teachings is conscience and the light of nature, we need all the aid that thought and language can give.

The question is often asked, "When shall I commence preaching?" The answer is easy; "After six months." Start with a sermonette or baby sermon; day by day add to it, and, if kept in motion, it will grow like a snowball rolled over the common. The best way of learning to preach is to preach. The first sermon a man who is the oldest Christian in the city heard was one which was preached when the speaker was not able to talk over five minutes. An old missionary said of juvenile efforts, "It will do no harm." He might have added, "It may do good."

In some fields attempts have been made to preach through an interpreter. The man who is called to a heathen land at threescore has no alternative, but not he who is half that age. Leaving out of question the difficulty of translating at the instant, the length of time required for a discourse twice spoken, and the difficulty of obtaining a reliable interpreter, the very fact that the foreigner lacks the "idiom of thought" stamps this method of speaking as essentially defective. Unless there is a mental affinity between the minds of the speaker and the hearer, to convey truth is a difficult task. A minister, through an interpreter, addressing an audience composed both of Christians and heathen, said: "A certain nobleman asked, 'What proof was there of the truth of Christianity?' and was answered, 'The Jews, my lord.'" To rightly interpret the reply would require a section of the world's history, and would take about two weeks. A Chinese Mandarin asked, "In America how do you choose a President?" A Consul answered, "We have two great political parties, the Republicans and Democrats. Each party puts up its candidate and the choice is between them." The interpreter said, "The country is divided into North and South; the North puts up one candidate and the South another." The difficulty lay in trying to say Democrat or Republican, or Whig and Tory, or Liberal and Conservative in Chinese. A bishop, on a recent visit to a neighboring kingdom, had for an interpreter the finest linguist in his mission. He was addressing the class for ordination and trying to impress upon them the necessity of giving more prominence to the sermon than to the exhortation. He said, "Strokes could be made with a lash, but they were harder if the lash was fastened to a stock—the sermon was the stock and the exhortation the lash." Our linguist could not think of the word "stock," or of a more suitable figure, so he said the sermon was like a dog and the exhortation as the tail, which, of course, carried as little meaning as that of a dog wagging his caudal appendage. It is better for a man to be his own interpreter. Those, however, who are so situated that they cannot do otherwise, let them use an interpreter.

Some, like Moses, speak effectively through the lips of another, and it may be a means of awakening attention, converting men, and building up the church in faith and knowledge.

An extensive acquaintance with the literature of the country is necessary for one who has a literary profession. It brings us into association with the brain of China. If we quote the authors the people honor, it adds much weight to our address. We must know something of Chinese philosophy and the leading teachings of the sages. Especially should ministers appreciate the high order of moral excellence inculcated in their books, and make this a basis for the higher truths of religion. A "working knowledge" of the classics is almost essential to our success as preachers. There is no department more necessary than a familiarity with the light literature of China. Very little of it will bear a full translation, because of coarse expressions in nearly every chapter, but it is easy to pass over these parts for the great benefit of reading semi-colloquial books. The collections of proverbs are very useful to those who master them. The native newspaper gives the current thought of the day, and the English "leading journals" at the port keep one in a Chinese atmosphere. There is a field for research in the standard English works on China, and those missions are wise which put them into the student's curriculum. The Chinese language is so constructed that it requires regular study—if only a short time each day—for a score of years, for if the one who uses the vernacular does not go forward he is apt to fall behind.

By close observation we are to obtain an insight into Chinese character. They are keen observers and form their estimate of the man who stands before them with surprising astuteness, and shall we be behind them in the study of men? This book of human nature in China is in many volumes, printed in divers copies and bound in a variety of styles; not all equally interesting, but a knowledge of the whole is beneficial and instructive. We come as teachers of the Bible, but if we follow the example of Jesus, we will preach the word of God in the language of men. As we are religious teachers we must, first of all, become acquainted with the three great idolatrous systems, as there is no finer field of illustrating the true than by comparing it with the false.*

---

* For the elucidation of this part of the subject, the reader is referred to the *Dragon, Image and Demon; or Confucianism, Buddhism and Taoism* and *The Three Religions of China*, published by A. C. Armstrong & Son, New York; S. W. Partridge & Co., London.

The Chinese do not exercise their minds on high topics, but they do know many small things. We must, like them, be intimately acquainted with the three hundred and sixty trades, and especially the prices of all commodities. When we are speaking, the markets, fruit stands and vegetable stalls must be on the tongue's end for the sake of illustration. A man must know how to build a house, row a boat, plant rice, irrigate the fields, rear the silk worm, weave silk and quarry stone! We are, in our linguistic attainments, to be scholars, merchants, cobblers, cooks, coolies and washermen. We must know what the people know, and prepare our sermons in the language of their daily life. It is desirable to be acquainted with the topography of our section of country, and the names of localities. A lady to reach the women must converse fluently on all the details of home life and woman's employments and avocations. What a vast field of research there is in the government of China, and how can we better show the eternal jurisdiction of Jehovah than by delineating a human system which has proved its stability by its centuries? Each one is appalled by the magnitude of the task, but daily strength comes by daily food, and our ability to speak lies mostly in the effort to prepare.

CHAPTER IX.

THE STYLE OF PREACHING.

THIS topic can best be introduced by the question, "Where are we called to preach?" The answer is immediately returned, "In the Orient." Then let the style of preaching be oriental. The first thing that arrests the traveller's attention in the East is the oriental style of architecture—the dragon comb to the roof, the ornamental cornices and quaint carvings. Or if in the stores we look at the finer class of goods, how many pretty things adorn the shelves, little cunning contrivances which please the eye but seem to lack in utility. Note the variety of fans which gentlemen carry in their hands and delight to admire! How many multicolored silks there are in a silk and satin hong! In China there are no factories on the gigantic scale of the West, turning out their fabrics by the bale, or car-load, or ship-load, but there is an endless variety of minor goods and chattels. When we come to the language we find that the whole idea is to write a pretty composition in a florid, high-flowing, ornamental style. As they are fond of talking, and spend so much time in conversation, their field of spoken language is so broad that we can never hope to cultivate more than one small corner.

The first thing that must be impressed upon our minds is, that the style of preaching here must be something distinct from the essays in English monthlies, or the ordinary mode of sermonizing. If the one thought is distinctly before the speaker, of preaching differently from what he would do at home, it is quite easy to find the right road. He must first leave the "old ruts," then he will blaze out a new route. In doctrine he is to "ask for the old paths," in the method of presentation he must in China search for the new.

We are to preach in a bright, lively style. The people are merry talkers, full of wit and quick at repartee, so our addresses must be in a happy strain. The poetic faculty must be cultivated so that illustration becomes second nature. The Chinese show great skill in the use of figures of speech in their ordinary conversation. They delight in the picturesque, and in all that adorns and beautifies. A graphic description arrests their attention, and we should guide them through the picture galleries of Scripture narrative, and sketch sacred scenes with the pencil of language. They appreciate the flowers of rhetoric and the polished gems of oratory. The native preachers are fond of analogy, and their gifts lie so decidedly in that line that it is difficult to keep their metaphors within just bounds. Dr. Guthrie, visiting a gallery on the continent, asked one who was present "What was his profession?" "An artist." "I too am an artist." "Ah!" quoth the stranger, in surprise. "I paint with words," said the gifted preacher. But some may reply, "Did not the apostle declare, 'And my speech and my preaching was not with enticing words of man's wisdom?'" True, but he did not mean that the ministry should make no effort at adornment in style, but that pretty language should not be the end and object of discourse. Paul would disclaim against collecting Chinese apothegms, striking proverbs, and classic quotations simply for the purpose of tickling the ears of those who hear. We are not to adorn the body of the sermon so that men will forget that there is a living soul within the form of words. We are not to preach rhetoric, but we may use rhetoric in preaching. If our style leads men to forget the cross and think only of the flowers in the pulpit, then our work is a failure, but if we can attract men to Christ by the choice use of words, then we have fulfilled our mission. Speaking in language too elegant is not a snare into which the European who talks Chinese is likely to fall.

We must preach simply. One of the greatest difficulties is to appreciate the profound ignorance of those whom we address, especially in the domain of religion. "Darkness shall cover the earth and gross darkness the people." If we inquire into their attainments in geography, an educated man is quite satisfied if he knows that America has a city called New York, a region denominated "The Golden Mountains," and formerly a great man named Washington. The first question in the infant catechism, "Who made you?" puzzles philosophers and sages. We make a speciality in the high and low sounds of this "great tonal tongue," of the monosyllabic idioms and of the rhythm of language, but no less should we aim at perspicuity in thought, and lucidity in the form of its presentation. It is the highest mark of the ability of a teacher to state profound truths in a simple way. We once saw a specialist in Natural History teach orally a number of children at the table the difficult nomenclature of the science, by giving some felicitous handle by which they might grasp each term. Compare the literary efforts of one who has been on the field five or ten years, in his translations of western theological works, and the simple primers in Christian truth the same missionary gives to the church after an experience of five and twenty years.

We are to preach *appropriately*. Our Saviour said, "Therefore every scribe which is instructed unto the kingdom of heaven, is like unto a man that is a householder which bringeth forth out of his treasure things new and old." The preparation for the home pulpit is made in the study, though many bright thoughts come to the extempore speaker during the time of delivery. The very motionlessness of the audience requires him to draw on his own resources, but with an ever varying congregation it is easy to find a fulcrum for the lever, or a pin on which to hang an illustration. There are so many sights and sounds which suggest thoughts that are "as goads and as nails fastened by the masters of assemblies." The preacher must be ever ready to take advantage of every felicitous event to turn it to good account. The springing rice, an emblem of the first blades of grace in the heart; the golden grain, ripe for the sickle, a symbol of "gathering in the sheaves"; the setting sun suggests a sermon to the old; the postman, who comes in the chapel, reminds the hearers of the gospel messenger with a letter from the Heavenly Father; the burden-bearer of the words of him who said, "Come unto me all ye that are weary and heavy laden"; the merchant collecting bills, of our settlement at the day of final accounts; the clanking chains of the passing prisoner tell us that we are all criminals. Starting on a direct line the speaker must be ready to vary his discourse so as to adapt it to every passing occasion, just as the boatman shifts his sails with the changing breeze or curving canal, or as he guides so skillfully his little barque as it shoots around the sharp angles in the rapids. He leaves his first topic just as a party of us in the Mammoth Cave, arriving at the river and finding it rising so rapidly that, did we cross, a safe return could not be insured, left the main course and turned into a side passage to behold some of the greatest wonders which are hidden beneath the surface of the ground. Our sermons must at times be like the shifting, varying reflections of the kaleidoscope, but, like this simple instrument, they must always reflect a beautiful picture.

Again, in preaching, it is important for our thoughts to run in native channels. Here must be undone much of the systematic teaching of our western schools, or rather we must adapt our learning and our logic to the circumstances by which we are surrounded, so that instead of the railway or steamer, we must travel by native boat in the native waters. There are Chinese channels of thought, and in these our discourse must run; there are intellectual pathways, and on these our minds must travel. We are not to despise the ditch-bank and compare it with the turnpike, for on this narrow causeway, water on one side and mire on the other, millions of men have trod. The idiom of thought is a most difficult acquisition, but by constant mental intercourse with men and books, we may obtain it. This is the key to the lock of their understanding. Revolve in their orbits and there is no friction. Note in the *Dream of the Red Chamber* the description of a rich man's house, not the green sward, royal oaks, and stately mansion, but horses at the door, sedans in an adjoining apartment, the side entrance for the servants, the multitude of ahmahs, the vegetables for the kitchen, and all the incidentals of a well-ordered household. Why tell of the prodigal in Judea, when hundreds of fathers in this city long for the return of spendthrift sons from Shanghai? Why talk of Grecian games within sight of the examination hall where the candidates seek for the "corruptible crown"? In what land can we better explain the "wicked husbandmen" than here, where many try to evade paying the "rent rice"? We must study our illustrations and jot down in a pocket note-book every new line of thought. We are not to bring our illustrations from a western land. It is not necessary to import our rice from Charleston or our sugar from New Orleans. To patronize the native market is better.

In preaching, the illustrations must be exact, or the Chinese will never catch the idea. They are bright enough if you tell it their way, but their imaginations will not follow us beyond the sea to the scenes of our childhood. It is easy, by the blank expression on their faces, to tell that the speaker has failed to convey the idea. To illustrate how Christ suffered in our stead, I often spoke of the two brothers in school, the elder diligent, the younger lazy, and when the latter was about to be punished by the teacher, the elder brother took his place and stood in a corner of the room for an hour. It never seemed to me the hearers appreciated the truth which I desired to present. One day, in a native school, I saw a boy kneeling at a bench. By changing "standing" to "kneeling" it fit like the lead in a mold. We must hit the target or the winged arrow fails in its flight. Some years ago I had my teacher write about the young Huguenot taking his father's place at the galleys for six years. He said, "I see your meaning; you wish to illustrate substitution, but the people will never catch your idea; they will say, 'Oh! yes, how filial he was.'" It is well to test the gun before taking it to the scene of action.

We must preach *slowly;* not talk slowly, but restrain our imagination and not let it fly at the speed of a lightning-express. The Chinese are not accustomed to the western style of public speaking as is heard in the pulpit and in political meetings, they cannot follow a rapid train of thought. As the natives say, "Slowly, slowly, go." The story-teller in the tea-shop alone carries on the several parts of a dialogue, and with his voice delineates the scenes which in the occident require several actors. He does not narrate his story in an unbroken strain, but asks a question and answers it himself. This double method of conversation, like the double-entry method in book-keeping, secures absolute accuracy,—the rule is to say everything twice, first in the form of interrogation and then in reply. This idiom is manifest in all Old Testament narratives, where the writers take twice as long to detail an event as in our modern writings. The biblical style is the model for preachers in Asia; study it, imitate it. The original is a pattern perfect in its conception and literary execution. The Jewish writers living before the time of Confucius, furnish us with the fashion plates of the modern Chinese vernacular.

Again, the truth must be preached clearly and distinctly. The Chinese are not accustomed to our methods of reasoning, or our logical processes. They move in a circle, as the buffalo at the water-pump, and we must patiently instil the truth into their minds and allow them to get one idea clearly before we present another. "For precept must be upon precept, precept upon precept; line upon line, line upon line; here a little and there a little." Foreigners often get irritated with servants for their apparent stupidity, whereas it is the fault of the one who gives the orders. We are to give our instructions minutely: "Go down the street. At the first corner turn to the left. You will come to a bridge. Do not cross the bridge. Go to the right till you come to a Zamen with two flag-posts. Then at the cross-street go southwards. Do you understand?" "Yes." "You will come to an open space with some trees. That is not where I send you. Go further on till you come to a tea-shop; it is a very large one with a tiger furnace facing the west. Just opposite is the chapel I want you to go to." "Oh! yes, I know, I can find it," and the man will not miss your instructions. Our directions to the traveller journeying to the gates of the Celestial city must be equally explicit.

Another important point is not in the first instance to state abstract truths, but to approach the subject in the natural line of thought. Ask an old woman, "Have you a soul?" and ten to one she will reply, "No." Mention that the people all say they have "three souls and six spirits," and inquire if this is the case. "Oh, yes, every one has three souls and six spirits." Then you may point out the error, and instil the truth.

In preaching, we must occasionally let the minds of the audience rest. Stop and talk on any common point, and the faces before us will immediately brighten. "Yesterday I went to the country. I took a boat. We passed down the canal, and through a bridge. The rice-fields looked green and beautiful. On the right bank were piles of water-jars. Soon to the left the hills were in sight. Then we came to Mohdoh. 'Old man, have you ever been to Mohdoh?' 'Yes, yes.' 'Well, then, you know all about it.' I met a man, and asked him the way up the mountain. We walked along the road together, and passed a grave. I said, 'My friend, do you know that the dead shall rise?'" This whole preamble, or verbal ramble, is totally irrelevant, but the hearers are on the *qui vive* to know what is coming.

In addressing those whom we meet, we are not to rush on them too suddenly. Accosting a stranger, we are not to shout, "There is one God and one Mediator!" We occasionally speak to strangers who say they cannot understand; so fully are they convinced that we are speaking in a European language, that they cannot understand their mother tongue. "My friend, where is your honorable residence?" "Waseih." "In the city or the country?" "Country." "How far from Waseih?" "Twenty *lee*." "What is your high longevity?" "Very little." "Well, how many years?" "Sixty-four." "How many sons have you?" "Two." "What are their ages?" "Twenty-six and eighteen." "The eldest is married, I suppose; you have a daughter-in-law, have you not?" "Yes." "Any grandchildren?" "A grandson." "I congratulate you." "I am unworthy." "Are you staying now at an inn, or with a friend?" "With a friend." "Near your home are there any temples?" "Oh, yes, many." "What are they?" "The god of agriculture and the goddess of mercy." "Any gods of the district?" "Plenty of them." "Do the people burn incense?" "Every first and fifteenth of the moon." "My aged friend, do you know that idolatry is a great sin?" "What!" You have this old man caught in the meshes of the gospel net, and his mind is prepared to hear the first truths of theology. Take the last chapter of John as the model of oriental discourse. Jesus waited till their hunger was satisfied, then conversed about love. Study the details as they are so simply given, and see how circumstantial the historian is. The whole of the fourth Gospel is a beautiful specimen of eastern literature, and the missionary is wise to imitate the Johannine style.

The first great essential is to wake them from the slumbers of four thousand years, and to sound the gospel alarm, "Awake, thou that sleepest, and arise from the dead, and Christ will give thee light." The people must be aroused from their lethargy and death-torpor. We come with the message that there are three great roads—the heavenly road, the human road, and the road of devils; that they have the two last, but not the first, and we beseech them to leave the third, and to walk in the way of heaven. They are accustomed to exhortations to virtue, and conceive of us only as teachers of morality. A resident at the port, speaking with me about preaching, said, "Of course you never say anything to offend them."

"Well, sir," was the reply, "if we did not, we would never get an idea into their heads." It will ever remain, "the offence of the cross." They listen, and say, "Oh, yes, honor father and mother; worship heaven and earth." Not that the message has not been pointedly delivered, but because they are preoccupied with the idea that there is nothing else besides father and mother, heaven and earth. It requires a shock from an electric battery to convince them that we have a higher message. I used to be troubled by hearing men who had listened to a discourse walk complacently out of the chapel, saying, "Oh, yes, all the same, worship heaven and earth"; but very seldom these last years, for whenever heaven and earth are mentioned I act, so to speak, like Paul and Barnabas at Lystra, when "they rent their clothes, and ran in among the people"; and so I shout, "Wickedness! Wickedness!! Wickedness!!!" They are dead to spiritual things, and will through a sermon mentally sleep with their eyes open, unless they are awakened as it were "with the voice of the archangel, and with the trump of God." Satan has administered opiates, and the case requires heroic treatment. They lie softly upon their beds while the flames roll around. Our preaching must be as if the earth were quaking beneath their feet. We must cry, yea, cry aloud, "Hear," oh, China! "The Lord our God is one Lord!"

Yet at the same time we are to be courteous, and to use every felicitous method of address that will enlist their sympathy. The Chinese excel in politeness, and shall we neglect to be gentle and affable, and by our courtesy try to win them? A short time since, a native preacher from a neighboring chapel said, "All on the streets are busy collecting their debts, but I would infer from the happy expression on the faces of the audience that you have all settled your accounts at the close of the year." We can always remark, "Do not get angry if I say something to you." "Certainly not, speak; I will be only too happy to listen;" and we can then talk with impunity about their most sacred institutions.

We note that the Chinese in conversation, from politeness, always "take the lowest seat." If then, in illustration, one of the parties is bad and the other good, one rich and the other poor, one the judge and the other the prisoner, should it be desirable to use "I" and "you," always let the speaker be the inferior and the hearer the superior. In this way the good-will of an audience may be secured and nothing lost in the effect the sermon will produce. Another method of preaching is "to tell how we do." How we daily pray; our family prayers; our Sunday services; how the Sabbath is kept in Christian lands, and everything in connection with the church. This is an unfailing source of interest, and to preaching in this style they cannot possibly take exceptions.

We are to unfailingly insist upon our credentials, that we are sent, not as they foolishly think, by a foreign emperor, but by the King of kings. Though we have no apostolic signs and wonders, we can testify what Christianity has done for the nations which have accepted its teachings. In this city, residing on High Market street, is a venerable Confucian preacher, now fourscore, who preaches two or three times a month in the temples or open courts. A table with a red cover hanging in front is mounted on two chairs, and on this lie his manuscripts. Dressed in satin robe and boots, and standing on another chair, he speaks to the forty or fifty who gather around. The *gist* of his orations is that certain who committed crimes or were guilty of great wrongs received the due reward for their evil deeds from heaven. Some of these incidents, or rather most of them, would be too coarse for a European audience. He speaks with much deliberation, and always begins by giving the name of the party, the place in which and the year when he lived. This particularization in the details and presenting proofs for the statements are evidently suggestions for preachers of the gospel.

Another mode of oral address, and the most effective one is *talking* versus *haranguing;* to adopt the "conversational, catechetical or Socratic method." This requires long and careful training and much practice, but opportunities must be sought for and improved. Some missionaries can deliver a whole discourse by questioning the audience and securing suitable replies. Sitting on the back of a bench and talking on spiritual subjects to thirty or forty who are gathered near, ten times as much truth will be conveyed as by an ordinary discourse. The difficulty is to find a good questioner. Again, they will start on religion and wish to pass to other topics and ask irrelevant questions about foreign civilization or the price of articles of dress, but when they ask about religion this method of preaching secures fixedness of attention and receptivity of the truth. When a number are fully interested, we may step upon the platform and speak with power. Truly we are to be all things to all men and all occasions, and always to do the best we can, and when talking in the chapel or on the street, momentarily seek for divine guidance. We are not invariably to follow the rule, "To speak to a scholar as to a scholar, and to a peasant as to a peasant," for we must remember that in theology the one is as ignorant as the other, and what suits the one will be adapted to the other, and from experience I can say that the scholars at the examinations listen to the most elementary truths with much interest. The philosopher and the coolie must alike sit at the feet of Jesus.

We notice that the Chinese in talking, when they are speaking on a topic which, they judge, might be unpleasant, state the converse, and leave the hearer to make the application. This is a fine way to state truth, and, if done with skill, no people are more ready to see the point and to apply it personally to themselves. They leave *unsaid* what we wish specially to say. It is beautifully illustrated in the tender reply of Cushi to David, when he asked, "Is the young man Absalom safe?" "The enemies of my lord the king, and all that rise against thee to do thee hurt, be as that young man is."

We have not only to learn the language, but our voices must be trained. Elocution must be a prominent department in missionary culture. Many of the story-tellers along the streets would be awarded medals for the naturalness with which they imitate all classes. So much accustomed are the Chinese to their historical plays and tea-shop recitations, that it comes almost second nature with most of them to change the tones of their voices as they repeat what others say. The voice is given us to attract men to Christ. The cry of a beggar wakes up a congregation. The hawkers on the street arouse their attention. The cry of the drowning sailor, "Save life! Save life!" brings them face to face with the grave. On my desk lay a manuscript about the riot at Ephesus. A Yamen secretary in the study picked it up, and read the speech of the town clerk, or *wei-yuen*, imitating to perfection a mandarin as he speaks to his runners. This almost every Chinaman can do. I heard a senior missionary, in relating an anecdote, imitate the pompous official, and in the next sentence the obsequiousness of the servant. This may be done in the pulpit so as to be ridiculous; again, the inflections of the voice may carry conviction to many a heart. We must speak with pathos, looking unto the rock whence we are hewn, and the hole of the pit whence we are digged. Never once excite a laugh, or the spiritual effect is lost.

At times truth is best conveyed by the eye, and

so the blackboard, the whiteboard, or scrolls may be successfully introduced. The text or topic with the principal thoughts written, and the comments spoken, may be "sharper than a two-edged sword, piercing even to the dividing asunder of soul and spirit." The Chinese use their characters so much for ornament, as on their sign-boards, or for wall-pictures, that this effective method may be well utilized.

We may go back three thousand years, and listen to the words of the wise man: "Because the preacher was wise, he still taught the people knowledge; yea, he gave good heed, and sought out and set in order many proverbs. The preacher sought to find out acceptable words." The missionary must seek for *acceptable* words—"illustration, proverb, quotation, interrogation, classical sayings." It is not to offer unto the Lord that which costs nothing mentally. As long as we live, each day special efforts must be put forth to present the truth so as to constrain men to accept the gospel. "With such a theme, let every power of the imagination, every facility of expression, every gift of utterance, be enlisted and employed." To show how the man of God, to the end of his days, must exercise himself in preparing for a heathen audience, the venerable Rev. William Muirhead, the preaching apostle of mid-China, the "old man eloquent," who for nearly a half-century has so fervently delivered his message daily, and usually many times a day, recently said: "I have been astonished beyond measure at the wonderful number of hearers with which I have been favored in the old Union Chapel. It is well situated, and especially at night crowds are passing to and fro, who are easily attracted. Altogether, it is a magnificent sphere for missionary work, and the burden on my soul is that of souls and *how most suitably to address the multitudes.*"

CHAPTER X.

Natural Theology.

WE now pass from the *how* to the *what*, from the *manner* to the *matter* of discourse. The preparation for the work and the style of preaching are very insignificant compared with the subject-matter. Again comes the question, "Where do we find ourselves?" The answer is returned, "Amidst one of the most idolatrous nations in the world." The great theme for the missionary is theology. It may be asked, "Did not the apostle to the Gentiles say, 'We preach Christ crucified,' and shall we not simply preach of Jesus and his love?" A glance at the fourteen epistles of Paul and the range of topics discussed within shows that he uses the term "Christ crucified" as the formula for the whole of revelation, giving special prominence to the doctrines of the blood. To the countries where the apostle travelled, the Jews had already gone and built synagogues, and it was known throughout the Roman Empire that there was a strange sect which held to theism in the midst of abounding polytheism. In China we have had no forerunners. The fundamental doctrine in reference to Christ is that he is the Son of

God. If a Mongolian, like the Ethiopian, confesses that Jesus is the Son of God, he is immediately baptized. Before we can preach about the Son of God we must let the people know who God is. To set forth the divinity of Christ we must first declare the "I Am." The beginning of religious knowledge is to know God. We cannot progress one step till we have settled the first, chief and great problem in divine science. The Gospels of Moses and John begin respectively, "In the beginning was God," "In the beginning was the Word." The devoted William Burns criticized the preaching of some missionaries that it was *too evangelical*, that is, they did not dwell sufficiently at first upon the evidences of Christianity. After this they were to go forward with the great truths of salvation and make every discourse point to Christ as the spokes to the axle.

Our task in answering the question, "What is God?" so that a heathen may comprehend that "God is a spirit, infinite, eternal and unchangeable in his being, wisdom, power, holiness, justice, goodness and truth," is a gigantic one. Take the Princeton theologian as he stood upon the mount of illumination, and his work was as nothing to ours. There sat in his lecture-room men who had college diplomas, were masters of several languages, and who accepted the Revelation, so the teacher could draw from wells older than Jacob's and from the newly discovered springs of knowledge, a school of young philosophers with the gates of faith and intellect all open. What have we? Ignorant idolaters. There are only a few narrow passes by which we can approach the ancient citidel of superstition. Shall we come first with the Bible as a witness and state its teachings about God? The people know not the Scriptures and accept not their testimony. What then is the basis of religious teaching in a heathen land? The apostle says, "For when the Gentiles, which have not the law, do by nature the things contained in the law, these having not the law are a law unto themselves: which shew the work of the law written in their hearts, their conscience also bearing witness, and their thoughts the meanwhile accusing or else excusing one another." The light of nature and the teachings of conscience are not obscure, for Paul says, "The invisible things of him from the creation of the world are clearly seen, being understood by the things that are made, even his eternal power and godhead."

The first inquiry that presents itself is, Is there a God? Gather in one mighty assembly all the gentry of China—the scholars, the philosophers, the sages, the wise men—and propound the question, Is there a God? and there will be the silence of the grave. Examine the tomes of antiquity, search the volumes which fill imperial libraries and we obtain no answer. Let the three religious systems, which have existed from two thousand to four thousand years, marshal their votaries, and what answer is given? Confucianism does not consider the question of the origin of the universe, Buddhism says boldly and decidedly there was no Creator, while Taoism is too busy with spirits and demons even to consider the question. To appeal to these cults is like addressing an audience of the deaf, dumb, and blind. There is, however, a feeble response when we appeal to individual hearts and consciences. We bid them look at their own souls; with the soul there is life; without it, they say, a man is dead. They are conscious of the domain of spirit over their own bodies; why should they not search for the Great Spirit that rules the universe? The soul of man reflects the image of the Creator, just as a glass of water the shining sun. If there be not the great "Father of spirits," whence come our spirits? Or consider the immortal mind, which in imagination can travel so far, in reasoning can climb to such heights, in breadth can feel such extremes of joy and sorrow—may we not think there is an infinite mind which controls heaven and earth? Or memory, so surprisingly developed by the Chinese system of education, the storehouse in which are laid up the treasures of knowledge; where is the source of this wonderful faculty? Whence cometh man's moral nature? Does not conscience, the invisible monitor that tells of right and wrong, point upward to an infinite source of moral action? An unanswerable argument is man's religious nature. Travelling over the earth, no matter to what clime we go, or what the condition of the race, men engage in the worship of a Being or of beings higher than themselves. Our religious nature demands an object of love and reverence, who can hear our confessions, praises, and prayers, and supply all our wants. Again, why do men look to God, or the gods, when they are sick? Why this visiting the temples, and supplicating the favor of the gods for those who are racked with pain? Does not the cry of helpless humanity point to One who can help? The seventh argument is drawn from the existence of the false. What is the counterfeit but an imitation of the true? Are not the tin-foil dollars, selling at three cents per one hundred dollars, to be burnt for the dead, fac-similes of the silver dollars? Are not the million false deities a witness of the One living and true God? Looking at man's moral, intellectual, and spiritual nature, the conclusion is irresistible, that it is only the fool that "hath said in his heart, There is no God."

From this the erring "offspring of God" may be led to read the book of nature, and to consider the relations of the great God to the universe about us. The important study for the missionary is, by careful analysis, to find out what the Chinese know, and to make this the basis for argument. To go beyond these, data may be instructive to the hearers, but the spiritual train of thought is lost, and what was designed for a theological discourse becomes a lecture on science. As they consider the pupil of the eye simply color, it would utterly bewilder their minds to tell them it is a window to let in the light. If we preach on Jesus, "the Light of the world," it is not necessary to tell of light coming in waves, or the rapidity of its travel, for the Chinese know as much about the subject as the Jews did when they heard of the "true light, which lighteth every man that cometh into the world."

Has, then, the universe a Creator? We stand upon the bounds of a mighty ocean; as far as the eye can reach there is the expanse of water; but this sea, which appears so boundless, has a shore which says, "Hitherto shalt thou come, but no further; and here shall thy proud waves be stayed"; so there must be a power which controls these worlds upon worlds. We see a hanging rope; it must be suspended on something, and may we not think that all things are upheld by the word of Jehovah's power? Everything we use has a maker: The house we live in, the table we write on, the chair we sit in, the bed we sleep on, were all made by some one. Look at a watch! Suppose it were found on an uninhabited island; I heard the tick, tick; I looked within, and beheld wheel upon wheel, each influencing the other, and all influenced by the main-spring, and regulated by the balance-wheel. The evident design of all this is to make the hands move, and mark time upon the graduated dial-plate." "The irresistible conclusion is, that some one made the watch." If it takes me days or weeks "to understand the mechanism of the watch, it must have been contrived by a still greater intellect than mine." The watch had a maker, and an intelligent maker. Such a watch is the solar system, and if we compare the movements of the sun with the watch, we find it "marking time with the utmost exactness upon the dial-plate of heaven."

And shall we not say the sun, moon, and stars—the "three lights," as the Chinese call them—must have a Creator?

If we come to a house, the reception-hall with handsome chairs and marble tables, the bed-rooms with finely-carved furniture, the study with its cases of books at the side, and pens and ink on the table, the kitchen with the viands all prepared—though we see no one, we conclude that the house has a master. Along the main street is a store with a golden sign, its entire front open, the goods lying upon the shelves, the clerks busy serving customers—though a stranger, I feel assured there is some one who owns the store. In the spring, on the commons, we see flocks of eagles and swallows flying in the sky, for the kites are exact imitations of the originals. If it is a proof of intelligence to make the kite, how much more to make the bird? Go to the weaver's and see the brocaded satin coming from the loom. First comes a practical artist, and lays out the warp. He arranges perpendicular threads, each in its place, and then his work is finished. Then the weaver uses his shuttle, and a little boy perched above pulls at the threads, and out comes the most beautiful embroidered silk. The pattern is a trophy of the designer's genius. Let us walk into a pleasure-garden, with its pavilions, and tea-houses, and bamboo groves, and flowering trees, and lakes, and labyrinthian rockeries. If these "false hills" were made by man, can we not think that the mountains show the Creator's power? We are to ask the people, Whence came the rice you eat for dinner? Last year's planting. And whence last year's rice? And from where the first grains of rice? If we ask where our bodies came from, the people answer, "From father and mother." And pray, from whence came father and mother? From ancestors, one generation above another. Then, how about the first father and mother? How naturally comes in the Scripture narrative.

While unfolding the true we have to combat the false philosophy of the Chinese as to the origin of the universe: That all things are self-produced; that heaven and earth, the great father and mother, originated all things; that the Great Monad was the primordial germ; that from the *yin* and *yang*, the male and female principles of nature, all things come; that the prime agent was the "lee," or "the principle of organization by which matter is preserved, or the power that inheres to direct it"; and that Pankoo divided the heavens and the earth. It is quite easy to show the absurdity of these vagaries.

The Chinese, like ourselves, are impressed with the glory of the celestial spheres, and an astronomical discourse is exceedingly appropriate. We are to point to the sun as the source of light and heat, and impress upon them how much they owe to the possession of these two blessings. We are to enlarge upon the beauties of the queen of night as she rides through the heavens. The stars, as diamonds in the sky, shine as brightly to the pagan as to the Christian. The pole-star, fixed in the north, here guides the mariner. While they wonder and admire, it is for us to show them that "The heavens declare the glory of God; and the firmament showeth his handiwork. Day unto day uttereth speech, and night unto night showeth knowledge. There is no speech nor language where their voice is not heard." The Chinese are so utilitarian in their views, and so much "of the earth, earthy," that they bow down, and worship "Mother Earth." The four seasons native artists love to paint, and of their beauty native poets delight to sing. The variety of fruits in the markets is a witness of the benevolence of Deity. The flowers the people love so, adorning the houses, courts, roofs, boats, and which the florist arranges so artistically in a mammoth bouquet, tell them that God has made a beautiful world for man to dwell in. The argument for use and the argument for beauty are both to be insisted on. The rainbow spanning the arch of heaven; the succession of hills and valleys; the diamonds, pearls, and precious stones; the goldfish in the artificial lakes; the little birds in the cages, which send forth joyful notes—these all tell how the Heavenly Father delights to please his earthly children.

The world is not thrown together at random, but order is the law of nature. The distribution of land and water; the deposition of dew which falls so gently with life-giving power on the thirsty earth; the fall of rain and "the snow from heaven," which "returneth not thither, but watereth the earth, and maketh it to bring forth and bud, that it may give seed to the sower, and bread to the eater," tell of an all-wise Providence. Is it a mark of prudent foresight to store away fuel for the winter? Then, what of the mountains of coal laid up for the ages! "If a father who, when he provides a home for his children, fits it up with all the necessaries and luxuries which they can possibly need, gives indisputable evidence of intelligence and love, then are those attributes to be ascribed to him who fitted up this world to be the home of his creatures."

The Chinese speak of the "five elements"—the

metals, wood, water, heat, and earth. What an amount of metallic substances in the Middle Kingdom! The mines of gold, the quantities of silver for commerce and ornaments, brass with its manifold uses, and iron in the mountains, lying just beside the coal. The forests supply materials to construct houses, boats, and furniture. How much water is used! For tea, cooking, bathing, washing, irrigating, and travelling! How many lakes, rivers, canals, and springs! Were the sea a halfmile higher, it would deluge the dry land. Ice expands in freezing, and so floats on top, and the fish are preserved underneath. Were water, like other substances, to contract by cold, it would sink, the canal become an iceberg, and all the fish die. How necessary to our existence is heat! We must also tell of the goodness of the Lord in providing the "five grains": God protects, farmers plant, boats transport, merchants sell, and men and beasts eat.

The physiological argument is one the people appreciate, for, though they know little of the muscles, they are acquainted with the bones and the important organs of the human system. Socrates called attention to the works of God, and pointed to the statue, so cold and immovable, as the highest display of man's art, and compared this with the figure, all warm with life, that can move, breathe, speak, and act, the handiwork of Jehovah. Let us visit a temple and see the idols sitting on their pedestals, big at the bottom and sloping upwards, and then see man, with the body large and tapering to the feet, his "four limbs and hundred parts" so supple and movable to turn, or stand, or sit, or recline. The thick head bones so assiduously guarding the brain, like the arch at the city gate; the beautiful curving column of the spine, giving flexibility to the body; the heart and lungs, enclosed by the ribs like the hoops around a bucket; the sockets of the joints, working so smoothly and not wearing out like the wooden hinges of a door, tell of wisdom in design. If the arms were as large as the legs, the weight would be oppressive; and if the legs were as small as the arms, man would be a monstrosity. The hand! Beasts have none; cats and dogs use their mouths; squirrels and monkeys their feet. Its skin fits like a glove. It has such a large number of bones and flexible joints, and turns at the wrist and at every joint! For writing, drawing, cutting, digging, the hand is used. Some machines are for coarse work, some for fine; but here is a machine which can build a house and mend a watch, pull a hempen rope and a silken thread, has a firm grasp and a delicate touch. How beautiful the human foot, with so many bones uniting to form an arch; and when the coolie carries a load, the weight it sustains is doubled!

Or take the eye. Is the camera a mark of skill and intelligence? It is made after the pattern of the organ of vision. The eye is protected by projecting bones, as Jerusalem was encircled by mountains. It has "the hedge of the eyebrows, the curtain of the eyelids, and the fence of the eyelashes." "The eye is not repaired; it repairs itself. It is not adjusted; it adjusts itself." It is moistened with tears, closed while we sleep, and open when we wake. "God has given to every man so high a value for his eye, and so quick an apprehension of danger, that no member of the body is more faithfully cared for than the organ of sight." The ear hears the loud peals of distant thunder, and the soft notes of music near at hand. The nose catches the sweet perfume of flowers, and also tells of decay, the removal of which prevents sickness. What a blessing is the gift of speech! The throat has "the windpipe" and "the food-pipe," with a trap-door over the former, which shuts when the food passes. We cut with our front teeth as with a knife, and grind with our back teeth as in a mill. The saliva is to moisten the food, and prepare it for assimilation. In a fever, the mouth is dry, because the heat, like the sun in a drought, dries it up. How wonderful the process of digestion! When we are weak, a bowl of rice gives strength, and prepares us for work. The lungs are the bellows, or "wind-boxes," and in them the blood meets with the air, and is purified. The most important organ is the heart, which acts like the system of water-works in Shanghai, playing the part of both the engine and the tower. How all the members of the body, framed together, form one complete whole! The eyes are not on the back, the ears on the breast, or the nose on the feet; nor are the important organs to be measured by their size, but "God hath tempered the body together." "If the whole body were an eye, where were the hearing? If the whole were hearing, where were the smelling? But now God hath set the members, every one of them, in the body as it hath pleased him."

Natural history presents its line of argument. How many varieties of birds in China, and in how many houses is there a cage with a pet songster, whose little room is kept clean, even though their own homes may not be in order. See the pheasant roaming wild in the fields around the city! Can the scholars along the streets, arrayed in silk, satin, and fur, be compared with one of these? God made the fowls of the air, with bodies small and bones light, a tiny bird carrying an immense wing. With what ease they sail aloft till we see but a small speck in the sky! Did man have wings, they must be as large as the side of the room, and he could not walk with such a load. What diversity there is in the bills of birds! The same is seen in their feet. Those of the woodpecker are like claws, and the duck's are web-footed. Watch the ease with which they swim! So the Chinese have taken the duck as the model for a boat.

The forests of the earth are a great zoölogical garden, and so extensive is the fauna that it is designated the "animal kingdom." Furs come from the snow-clad regions of the north, where beasts are provided with thick clothing. Dogs and tigers have sharp teeth to eat flesh, horses and cows broad ones to feed on grass. Man's throat is smooth, so that food slips down; the horse's throat is rough, so he can draw food upwards. As the elephant's neck is short, he is provided with a trunk, which is a weapon of immense power, and so delicate at the end that it can pick up a needle. In Central Asia they do not cross the sandy deserts in boats as in South

China, or in carts, as in North China, but on camels. Within the camel are fourteen bags, in which he stores water for the "dry and thirsty land where no water is." These facts lead the minds of the hearer to nature's God.

As we pass through the country we are struck with the quantities of fish. Along the coasts we see lights from the fishing boats; the rivers, lakes, and canals are full of them; fish nets and traps are everywhere to be seen. Perhaps millions obtain a livelihood from the waters. There are fish-hongs, and fish-stands, and fish-mongers. To raise sheep, hogs, and fowls takes money, but here is a costless provision of meat for the multitudes in this "hive of nations." There is no more patent fact than this of God's care for men. Then what a wonderful organism the fish is! Let a man be put under the water, and it fills his eyes and mouth, and soon he drowns; but the fish lives and moves. With his tail he skulls his own boat, just as the boatman uses the oar at the stern. His bones are fine and elastic, his fins are like the side wheels to a steamer, and his blood, colder than man's, is just the temperature of the water. What a sermon the fish is! How God has made all things so fitted for their special state! Were the horse the size of the dog, man could not ride; were the cow as huge as the elephant, it would not be suitable for the dairy; if the cat were as large as the hog, when wild it would be formidable; were the eagle of the dimensions of the mule, it could carry off men to its nest. See how the feet of horses, monkeys, and ducks are suited respectively for walking, climbing, and swimming! Fish are in the water, beasts on the earth, and birds in the air. Fish are not on the land, beasts are not in the air, nor birds in the water. Fish have scales, beasts hoofs, and birds wings. Beasts have not wings, nor fish hoofs, nor birds scales. The beasts of the field, the fowls of the air, and the fish of the sea are a happy triad that wait upon their Maker. "He causeth grass to grow for the cattle." "The cedars of Lebanon, which he hath planted, where the birds make their nests." "This great and wide sea, wherein are things creeping innumerable." "O Lord! how manifold are thy works! in wisdom hast thou made them all."

If natural theology teaches the existence of God, it may be asked does it tell of his unity, or is this a doctrine of Revelation as when God's chosen people learned their great lesson that Jehovah was one? Here are millions of gods. How are we to demonstrate to the Chinese that God is one? In answering this question. Mencius may be quoted, "Heaven has not two suns, nor the people two rulers." If it is necessary for a country to have only one ruler, how much more for the universe to have one king? During the Taipine rebellion, with two emperors, mid-China became a desolation and a ruin. As we behold how heaven and earth move in peace and union, we may know there is only one power that directs. Were there two gods, one might desire cold and the other heat, one winter and the other summer, one rain and the other sunshine. The four seasons would be in confusion, and heaven and earth overturned! Were there two, they must divide jurisdiction and so have limits to their power, but the essential idea of God is that he is illimitable. Were we to see a steamship built in different shops, the various parts when put together making one complete whole, would we not say that the models were designed by one architect? When the wooden frame-work of a Chinese house, built in the shop, is erected, and it is found that mortise and tenon, joint and socket fit the one to the other, is it not evident that the draught was made by one carpenter? We see everything made with some special design: the clock to keep time, the loom to weave, the boat to travel. Throughout creation it is also evident that one thing is designed for another. If air was heavier or lighter, birds could not fly; so he who created the birds created also the air. If water were more or less dense, fish could not live. He who made the fish made also the water. If all nations were governed by the same laws we would consider that there was one emperor. Does not the uniformity of the laws of nature point to the unity of God? The sun rises in the east and sets in the west. The moon and stars shine by night. The four seasons come in regular succession. A day and a night are twenty-four hours long. Were night to continue for three days it would be an Egyptian plague. If one was hot and the next cold, no constitution could stand it. A family, a boat, a house, a hong, each has its head, why should the universe be headless? The county has a district magistrate, the department a prefect, the province a governor, two provinces a viceroy, the eighteen provinces an emperor, and who above him? Men answer, "heaven." And who rules heaven? "O! Lord, our Lord, how excellent is thy name in all the earth! who hast set thy glory above the heavens."

The Bible teaches the Christian that "God is love"; the book of nature also tells the heathen the blessed truth of the Fatherhood of God. If there are seventy or eighty to eat from one kitchen, as in the large families in China, how much care to its head to provide? Then think of the race of men living on God's bounty! He supplies his children with furs for the winter, cotton for the spring, hemp for the summer, and silk for the fall. He gives them brass and iron, gold and silver. They have horses, cows, sheep, and hogs. On a bright spring day how happy creation is—the birds sing, the lambs sport, calves and colts play, and all living things seem happy! If all flowers had the same color, all birds the same feathers, all scenery the same appearance, all food the same taste, how monotonous! Man with his eyes sees pretty colors, with his ears hears delightful harmonies, with his palate enjoys pleasant tastes. Famines are the exceptions and years of plenty the rule, sick days only now and then and days of health continuous, days of sorrow few and our happy days many. Were the heavens paper, and the sea ink, and all the trees and woods pens, if we attempted to write of the goodness of God, the forests would be felled, the oceans dry, and the scrolls finished, and still we could sing "God is Love."

Day after day, during the epochs of creation, it

was recorded, "And God saw that it was good." Nature tells also of the perfection of God's works. Nearly everything done by man has some defect, but not so with the works of Jehovah. The sun is one, not two. Were there two the light would blind our eyes, and the heat would make the earth a furnace. In the early morn when the shadows roll down the mountain sides, and the rising sun gilds the east, and peak and headland are lit up, the dew sparkling upon the green leaves, and the birds with their first notes are heard, does not nature sing its Maker's praise! Men love to gaze at the moon, but were it brighter they could not enjoy its soft beams. If the light of the stars were more brilliant we could not rest at night. "Lo, these are parts of his ways; but how little a portion is heard of him!" Natural Theology tells us that there is a God, that he is one, that he is good, and he is almighty. This is the first outline of thought we present, and it is the door by which we may lead the pagan into the glorious temple of revealed theology and unfold the self-existence, eternity, omnipotence, omniscience, omnipresence, justice, goodness, truth and holiness of Jehovah. When we attempt to tell a poor heathen of the glory of God, we must, like the Seraphim, cry, "Holy, holy, holy, is the Lord of hosts: the whole earth is full of his glory." Where can we better speak of "God is a Spirit" than in China amidst the hosts of images and image worshippers? Or of him as the Living God than where it is the worship of dead men, and where in the temples "Death reigns?" To the Gentiles we present the internal evidences of our holy religion, and show them how the heart's desire to worship, and the truth that God is the object of worship fit the one to the other, as the two halves of a Chinese cheque, one of which is sent to the bank and the other to the party that collects. The sinner's wants are made known in prayer; God hears prayer. Here is the lock and its key. There are sins which I confess; God forgives sin. Does not one match the other, as the page of a book the stereotype plate from which it was printed? So we, as wise master-builders, use gold, silver, and precious stones, and to establish the truth of our holy religion draw our arguments from the heaven above, the earth beneath, and the consciousness of man. Thus with David we may sing the first part of the nineteenth Psalm, as the Gentiles ascend unto the hill of the Lord to study his word, and discover that "The law of the Lord is perfect, converting the soul: the testimony of the Lord is sure, making wise the simple." If the witness nature bears to the existence of God is so full, what must the Bible be which he has written to reveal his glorious attributes! If natural religion is such a grand field of research, what a wide domain for the preacher to the heathen is revealed theology!

CHAPTER XI.

The Light of Ethics and the Darkness of Sin.

THE apostle says of the Gentiles, "Which shew the work of the law written in their hearts, their conscience also bearing witness." As ethical teachers we are to study the moral code of the people to whom we come. One reason of the nation's longevity is the most excellent system of moral philosophy, known as Confucian, which is studied by every little boy who enters school. The silver rule of the sage, enunciated twice in different words, is the golden rule in a negative form, and with the same meaning. The exhortation of the philosopher Yientsze, whose temple stands in Soochow, "Love men," "Learn the doctrine," is an approach on the human side to the fulfilling of the law in the one word, "Love." The people speak constantly of "faithfulness, reverence, chastity, and morality" as the four pillars of the temple of Morality, and of the "five virtues," "benevolence, righteousness, propriety, knowledge, and faith," as the guiding principles of national integrity. In the doctrine of the man "the standard of excellence is placed so high as to be absolutely unattainable by unaided human nature." The author "probably intended to elevate the character of his grandfather to this height, and thus hand him down to future ages as the perfect and holy man. He has, in the providence of God, done his countrymen great service in setting before them such a character." "Compared with the precepts of Grecian and Roman sages, the general tendency of the writings of Confucius is good, while in adaptation to the society in which he lived, and their eminently practical character, they exceed those of western philosophers. He did not deal much in sublime and unattainable descriptions of virtue, but rather taught how the common intercourse of life was to be maintained."

Mencius speaks of "the heart which approves and disapproves," *i. e.*, conscience. He also says, "Without a heart to approve and disapprove, one cannot be a man." There are scores of proverbs about conscience, and in ordinary conversation the people appeal to their consciences. A common topic is the "heart." Without a "pious heart" worship is in vain; we are to "rectify the heart"; "the heart must be placed in the centre," *i. e.*, control all our actions. The teachings of the sages have been handed down through the ages, and have become part of their moral warp and woof. They boast of their ethical teachings, and we may change the words of Paul about the Jews so as to read, "Behold, thou art called a Chinese, and resteth in the law, and makest thy boast of Confucius, and art confident that thou thyself art a guide to the blind, a light to them which art in darkness, an instructor of the foolish, a teacher of babes." Some of the Parisees asked Jesus, "Are we blind also? Jesus said unto them, If ye were blind, ye should have no sin; but now ye say, we see; therefore your sin remaineth." It is the claim of the Chinese to high moral culture which makes them "without excuse." They say that western nations excel in arts and sciences, but that we have the literature and moral teachings. Often in the chapels, when we are speaking of duty, some stranger takes up the thread of discourse and talks both eloquently and pointedly. They converse with a glib readiness on these topics, and their words indicate a surprising knowledge of the true and the good. We are to recognize all that we find praiseworthy in the Confucian economy, but at the same time show the superiority of Christianity as a moral code, besides the glorious teachings on religion, on which topic the sage was silent.

Throughout the Bible, prominent doctrines are taught by contrast. So in China we may put their theoretical knowledge of morality over against their practical ignorance of sin. We do not come to a barbarous people to teach them the first principles of right and wrong, but to a nation highly cultivated in literature and the arts. We come to instruct them in the matter of salvation. By what avenue shall we approach them? How shall we tell them of Jesus, the Saviour of the world? It is evident they must feel their need of salvation before they can accept the mediation of Christ. To hear of religion as it is written in the books pleases them; it is redemption applied to their individual consciences which is so difficult. Our Master says, "The whole need not a physician." The Chinese, in their own estimation, are whole; even the prisoners in the gaols claim to be good men. Christ said, "I came not to call the righteous." The Chinese are *righteous*. The land is full of Laodiceans, who say, "I am rich, and increased with goods, and have need of nothing; and know not that they are wretched, and miserable, and poor, and blind, and naked." Shall we tell them of the love of God? They are delighted with the doctrine, and consider themselves the worthy recipients. We speak of the goodness of

God in providing food for his creatures. "Yes, the rice I eat is my due; I ought to have it; I am entitled to it; it is my own." We tell of the death of the Son of God. It is a panorama, a pretty picture, a wonderful spectacle of divine mercy. We say that Christ died for sinners, and they accept the statement as a general truth which has no application in the premises. The preacher asks, "Do you know what sin is?" "Oh, yes: murder, arson, robbery." "Have you any sin?" "Yes, everybody has sin." "Have you any personal sin?" "No, I have never done anything wrong." "Have you never had a bad thought?" "How could I? My heart is pure." "Has no profane word ever passed your lips?" "Never; I do not curse." "But in your early years did you never commit sin?" If I did, I have forgotten it; it makes no difference now." To hear them tell it, the Chinese are a sinless people. Day by day we converse with old men and old women who consider themselves immaculate. Others deem it such a small matter, that it is not worth talking about. Many are insulted by the question; the possibility of thinking I have sin!

This estate of Confucian perfection is almost incomprehensible to us. We speak of conviction of sin as it is felt sometimes during a powerful revival of religion, and perhaps in our own souls we have experienced the terrors of sins unforgiven; but from our childhood we have never been without a sense of sin; we have always had tender consciences, and, in a greater or less degree, have felt that sin is evil in God's sight. In Christian lands this is almost universal. Men who remain without the pale of the Christian church confess themselves to be sinners, and acknowledge that they personally have been guilty of sin. Those at home who deny that they have sin are just as scarce as men here who confess that they are sinners. People speak to us about praying to our Heavenly Father: "I suppose you kneel and say, 'Oh, Lord, here I am; I have a good conscience; I have never done anything wrong.'" The Saviour puts it exactly: "The Pharisee stood and *prayed thus with himself*" (all about *ego*), "God, I thank thee that I am not as other men are." They wipe their mouth, and say, "I have done no wickedness."

There are several causes of this self-satisfaction. In Zechariah's vision of the myrtle trees, those who rode upon the horses, answered the angel of the Lord and said, "We have walked to and fro through the earth, and behold, all the earth sitteth still and is at rest." "Thus saith the Lord of hosts. . . . . I am very sore displeased with the heathen that are at ease." The Chinese are the most contented people on the face of the earth, and they carry complete serenity (heart-ease) into the domain of religion. Another cause is their excessive worldly-mindedness. They "love the world and the things of the world." The love of gain is the one absorbing interest of their lives; so, with their thoughts fixed on this, they never look within. A third reason is their belief in the essential goodness of human nature. Their philosophy inculcates it, their teachers teach it, their scholars believe it, and the people accept it; so the doctrine that "all have sinned and come short of the glory of God" is a strange dogma. Again, the systems of merit have had a deadening effect upon the hearts and consciences of the people. Burning incense is not so much an act of worship to the gods as a method of gaining merit for man. Benevolent actions, fasts, vegetable diet, pilgrimages, are all meritorious; so a Chinaman is not "poor in spirit"; he is rich in merit. In the fifth place, their *political preaching* tends to make them have comfortable views of their own condition. The ministers of Confucianism speak only of the great crimes, and men who are guilty of these are publicly punished by heaven. The Yamen runners and hard-hearted publicans at the barriers are bad people; but the merchant of tolerable honesty; the teacher who is regular in his instructions; the lady who enjoys the money and fees the priests; the servant, who performs the simple chores—what wrong thing do they do?

Last year there was a proclamation posted throughout the city, naming 176 men who have formerly been before the police court, and telling them if they are again found guilty, they will be branded on the cheeks. The people have attentively read this document, and conclude that there are thus 176 bad men in Soochow, and 499,824 good people.

Again, Satan has murdered these people. Soulless gods have made soulless worshippers. They are dead, dead, dead! We astonish them when we affirm that the Pearly Emperor is not in heaven; when we say that the worship of heaven and earth is an abomination; when we assert that Jesus is the Lord of lords. These are small surprises. The startling fact is when they find themselves guilty sinners before the bar of an offended God.

A seventh reason is presented. Though they speak so fluently about moral responsibility, they have "their conscience seared with a hot iron."

Their sensibilities are deadened to eternal things. An illustration is seen in the back and legs of a peasant, the one uncovered to the suns of forty summers, and immersed, as the other has been, in the mud of the paddy-fields, the skin has become hardened by exposure; and so, in a measure, the sense of feeling is blunted.

It is evident the case needs heroic treatment. The love theory will not suffice. The minister is to preach the law. Paul gives us a section of his experience, "Nay, I had not known sin, but by the law. . . . For without the law sin was dead. For I was alive without the law once; but when the commandment came, sin revived and I died." His death, however, was to live again. "The law was our schoolmaster to bring us to Christ." It may be asked, Did not the Moravians pursue this policy, preaching about sin and the judgment, with no converts, but when one told the story of God's love many believed? True, but would the gospel have been accepted by the Icelanders had they not first heard the law? We are to lead the Chinese into the desert of Arabia, "to the mount that might not be touched, and that burned with fire."

"Awaked by Sinai's awful sound,
My soul in bonds of guilt I found."

Upon this citadel the preacher must level his heaviest batteries. It is not simply to drive a Chinese out of idolatry, that refuge of lies, but to drive him out of his self-righteousness, to make him know that robes of silk are the vestments of one who, "from the sole of the foot even unto the head there is no soundness in it; but wounds and bruises and putrifying sores." The people are surrounded by walls as high as heaven, and no Jonathan with his armor-bearer can scale them. We must not only make a breach, the fort must be leveled to the ground. To the human eye these bulwarks are impregnable, but the Holy Spirit will come as a "rushing mighty wind," a cyclone, and demolish the strongholds of Satan. The Comforter "will reprove the world of sin, and of righteousness, and of judgment." Then will they be "pricked in their heart." And what mourning! "And I will pour out upon the house of David, and upon the inhabitants of Jerusalem, the spirit of grace and of supplications; and they shall look upon me whom they have pierced, and they shall mourn for him, as one mourneth for his only son, and shall be in bitterness for him, as one that is in bitterness for his first born." "In that day" of mourning and prayer "there shall be a fountain opened to the house of David and to the inhabitants of Jerusalem for sin and uncleanness." If any experience has been gained during a ministry of some years, I would say, *Preach on sin.* Conviction of sin is the rugged path that leads to the "fountain filled with blood." The people stay away from Christ *because*—

> "The only fitness he requireth
> Is to feel your need of him."

Let us lead them to the garden of Eden, that earthly paradise, where our first parents were placed on probation, and let them in contrast behold the sad picture of the fall and all its direful consequences. They are to know the ways of sin. "Wherefore, as by one man sin entered into the world, and death by sin; and so death passed upon all men, for that all have sinned." The enumeration must be minute; sins of thought, word, and deed—"body, mouth, and heart," as they express it—sins great and small, accidental and besetting, secret and open, omission and commission; that we sin yearly, monthly, daily, hourly, momentarily; and of the wrath of God "revealed from heaven against all ungodliness and unrighteousness of men who hold the truth in unrighteousness."

A few years' experience will enable one to illustrate the dishonesty that pervades the social fabric; the divers weights and measures; the "squeezes" in making purchases for others; the extortion in the government offices, and the want of rectitude in financial transactions. To enlarge upon the sins of speech, of their facility in unblushing lies, and also of the fearful amount of profanity that proceeds from the lips of men, women, and prattling children. "their throat is an open sepulchre; with their tongues they have used deceit; the poison of asps is under their lips : whose mouth is full of cursing and bitterness."

Sin is to be compared with debt; and where is the Chinaman without debt? The magnitude of the debt is like the servant who owed 10,000 piculs of silver, or like the late banker Ho, of Hangchow, who, at the time of his death, was due the government sixteen million taels. Sin is to be presented as a disease, which affects the whole body, is universal, is handed down from our parents, and which the physicians cannot cure. The dreadful character of one single sin must be spoken of. One link broken, and the chain is broken; with one crack the mirror is ruined; one wheel out of order and the wheel stops; the pirate one robbery, and the murderer one victim, and the death warrant is signed; so every sin deserves

God's wrath and curse. Men are "dead in trespasses of sins"; hands unable to perform a right action, feet that cannot walk the heavenly road, ears deaf to the message of salvation, eyes that cannot see the truth, hearts which are unable to believe, just as the paralytic brought by four men to Jesus. Here in China is the valley in which Ezekiel saw the bones, "and behold! there were very many in the open valley; and lo! they were very dry." Six times are the words of Isaiah, which were quoted by Christ to explain the parable of the sower, used in Scripture. "By hearing ye shall hear, and shall not understand; and seeing ye shall see, and shall not perceive: for this people's heart is waxed gross, and their ears are dull of hearing, and their eyes they have closed; lest at any time they shall see with their eyes and hear with their ears, and should understand with their heart, and should be converted, and I should heal them." Jesus said to the Jews, "Ye are of your father the devil, and the lusts of your father ye will do. He was a murderer from the beginning, and abode not in the truth, because there is no truth in him. When he speaketh a lie, he speaketh of his own; for he is a liar, and the father of it." As a matter of observation, I never have such fixed and earnest attention from a heathen audience as when the topics are "dead in sin" and "children of the devil."

He, "the prince of the power of the air," seems to hold special control over the hearts and minds of the Chinese, and the nation is peculiarly under his dominion. Where upon the face of the earth has devil-worship assumed such multiform and divers kinds of homage? The very intellectual ability of the people seems keenly alive in considering the relations of spirits to men, and their ingenuity is taxed to the utmost in devising ways and means to ward off the attacks of the legions of devils. The gospel preacher is to study the scores of chapters of Holy Writ which denounce the fearful sin of idolatry. Though taught by patriarch and prophet, Israel would not learn the great lesson of her national life till after the captivity. How often were the chosen people punished and their cities laid waste just for this one sin! By what figures of speech did the writers of old, inspired by the Holy Ghost, describe leaving the ordinances of Jehovah and following after false gods? There is danger that men, from sympathy for the unfortunate pagan, lose their jealousy for the glory of Jehovah, and forget the fearfulness of the crime and the guilt of the perpetrators. God, in the moral law, describes idolaters as "those that hate me." Ezekiel tells of the 'images of their abominations," and Peter speaks of the "abominable idolatries." What a fearful picture the former gives us of the "wicked abominations" "portrayed upon the wall" "in the chambers of his imagery"! The condition of Peking is just as abhorrent in the eyes of the Most High as was that of heathen Rome as it was described by the apostle to the Gentiles. "Professing themselves to be wise, they became fools, and changed the glory of the incorruptible God into an image made like to corruptible man. . . . Who changed the truth of God into a lie, and worshipped and served the creature more than the Creator. . . . And even as they did not like to retain God in their knowledge, God gave them over to a reprobate mind, to do those things which are not convenient." As heathenism is the ancestor of vice, the aggravated guilt of the idolater must be fearfully set forth. The axe must be laid at the root of the tree if the way is to be prepared for the glorious advent of the Messenger of the Covenant.

CHAPTER XII.

PREACHING CHRIST.

AFTER the death of the proto-martyr the persecution waxed hot, and the disciples fled from Jerusalem. "Therefore they that were scattered abroad went everywhere preaching the word. Then Philip went down to the city of Samaria, and preached Christ unto them. And the people with one accord gave heed unto those things which Philip spake." The servants of the Most High follow the example of the evangelist and preach Christ, his person and glory. Protestants are denominated in China the "Jesus' Church," and as this sign is over our chapel doors the people ask, "Who is this whom you preach?" We give an account of the life and character of our Lord, telling how he preached the gospel, gathered disciples, performed miracles, and blessed mankind. The inquiry comes, must our teachings be drawn entirely from the gospel narrative, or are there intuitions in the Chinese mind and factors in their national economy by which we can illustrate the prominent features in the history of the Man of Galilee? We can answer in the affirmative that there are facts in their patriarchal institutions which stand as pulpit-rocks for the preachers of the new religion. Amidst the fearful array of difficulties which confront the advancing pickets it is a matter of devout thankfulness that in the government and social customs of this nation, which has survived the march of centuries and the wrecks of kingdoms, there are fundamental principles on which we may base our expositions. In going to any pagan country we expect to find false gods and to tell the people of the true God, but in Sinim we may tell there is "One God," and also find a basis for our teachings concerning the "One Mediator between God and man."

Christ the Mediator.

It is a privilege to set forth the mediatorial character of Christ in thought and language that the people daily use. The whole structure of the Chinese social and political economy is based upon the use of the "middle-man." No one thinks of employing a servant unless there is some one to recommend him, and the party recommending is held responsible for any misdemeanors of the underling. A stranger with no one to stand his security would not be able to get a position in any respectable family. A clerk would not apply for a situation in person—he would be rejected if he did—but requests a friend who is an acquaintance of the merchant to intercede in his behalf. Often the friend cannot do this directly, but speaks to a third party who has influence with the employer. No youth is allowed to enter the examination hall without having a former graduate—an alumnus of the college of letters—to act as security for his good behavior. In the important business of marriage the contracting parties have no voice in the matter, and their future destiny is in the hands of go-betweens. In renting a house a tenant does not seek the landlord, but the whole transaction is conducted by trusty intermediaries. The title-deeds to real estate have the names of the negotiators and of the one who stands security written upon them. Business in the government offices is transacted by influential friends who have the ear of the official. There is a graduated scale of fees for all of these services.

In the department of religion there are examples of mediatorship. The kitchen-god at the old year is supposed to ascend to heaven and tell the Pearly Emperor of all that the family has done during the twelve months; and they, by sweetening his lips as he starts upon his journey, hope to secure a favorable report of their deeds. Near the temple of the Pearly Emperor is a smaller one for the mediator of hades. The worshipper first goes to the shrine, burns incense, and requests him to intercede above and obtain permission for him to worship the god of gods. Even when the smaller gods come to pay their respects to the highest in the pantheon, they first go before the mediator and ask him to obtain for them an audience before Jupiter Optimus Maximus.

So common is the employment of middlemen, and so simple is the thought, that the Chinese accept it as a first-truth. We are often asked, "If we join your church must we have some one to act as surety?" and the direct answer includes the great fundamental principles of salvation. That Christ would stand as bondsman for a stranger or for a sinner fills them with surprise. Nearly the whole of the Redeemer's work can be presented under this—to the Chinese—simple concept. His standing between God and man, his pleading our cause, his acting as the mediator of the new covenant, his offering up our prayers, his opening the gate of heaven, his pledge of eternal rest, can all be expressed in such simple terms that a little Chinese child comprehends the meaning.

The Federal Headship.

In no country can the doctrine of Christ the Head of his redeemed be so fully illustrated as in China. Many reasons have been assigned for the stability of Chinese institutions and of the government that has stood for forty centuries, but of these, second to none is the federal relation between prince and subjects, or the legal responsibility of the one for the other. When Christ became the shepherd of his sheep—for whom he died—he assumed all their obligations and stood before God as their sponsor. The race of believers were grouped under a federal head and representative. It was a responsible undertaking, but in the acceptance and performance of this responsible trust lies the hope of the redeemed. The civic code of the middle kingdom abundantly illustrates the principle of representation, this prominent doctrine of revelation.

In China there is a legal unity between the governor and the governed. The Mandarin is held responsible for all that occurs within his territory. If there is a murder, the alternative is to find the murderer or lose his office. Blood is required where blood is shed, and till the man-slayer is produced, the official is not held guiltless. The rulers are the fathers and mothers of the people, and are accountable to the Emperor, not only for the faithful discharge of their personal duties, but for the peace and quiet of their subjects. If there is a disturbance or an insurrection, the theory and practice is that his rule should have been so wise and watchful as to prevent these demonstrations of violence. The fact that he is amenable for the acts of those within his jurisdiction makes the Mandarin doubly guarded in his administration. They are not forced to take office, but voluntarily assume these responsibilities. If there is a theft, in case the stolen property is not recovered, the *tipao*, or constable, is bambooed. This holding the policeman, or protector of the peace responsible for all that occurs in his ward, tends much to maintain good order.

Two years ago, as the manacles were removed from the prisoners at China New Year, by overpowering the wardens, ten robbers—two of them noted ones—escaped from the prefectural gaol. The only notice the provincial governor took of the case was to take away the Prefect's button. The alternative was to catch the fugitives or leave his office in disgrace. The matter touched the hearts, the pockets, and the positions of two hundred men in the Yamen, and there was great excitement. The Prefect offered $10,000—$1,000 a head—for their arrest. The whole energy of the Yamen was directed to catching the convicts, and messengers were dispatched to their respective homes. The soldiers and the police were active, and in a short time nine out of the ten were captured. The Prefect's insignia of rank were immediately restored. In Chinese law the jailer was not the responsible party in the first degree, but his chief, who is the governor of ten counties.

In the Northwest a private soldier during a long period stole, a little at a time, a quantity of lard which was entrusted to his charge, to the value of ten or fifteen dollars. It was afterwards discovered and brought to the notice of the Board of War. The soldier was beaten, his captain cashiered, the colonel removed, and the general censured. Why? There was clear proof of a lack of discipline in the army.

Some years ago a leading American house sent forty-four shoes of sycee into the Chehkiang province to buy tea, and they were stolen on the road. The firm informed the Consul, the Consul dispatched the Taotai, the Taotai informed the Futai at Hangchow, and he simply arrested the presidents of two boat hongs. Their families made inquiries on what boats the silver was carried, sent runners to the homes of the boatmen and found forty-two pieces buried beneath their beds. The heads of the boat companies were responsible for the acts of the sailors.

A year ago the son of the compradore of the French Bank in Shanghai tried to get Taels (200) from his father to pay an indebtedness. On his refusal the son invited the party to whom he owed the money to a tea-shop and asked for an indefinite time in which to pay it, and when the latter declined the lad shot him dead, and then blew out his own brains with the same pistol. After allowing the father due time to recover from the shock, the Taotai and District Magistrate, in view of this bloodshed, made him financial overtures. As his property was in danger he, under advice from the manager of the bank, offered by telegraph to Ti Hung Chang a subscription of Taels (10,000) for famine relief, if he would secure him against the squeezes of these two Mandarins. The offer was accepted, and the officials were chagrined to find themselves powerless to fleece such a fat sheep. Their indictment was, "You, as a father, failed in training your son, and so are responsible for his misdemeanors."

The subject may be indefinitely illustrated. When we speak of Jesus as the representative of his people, of his standing for them in the covenant of grace, of the whole responsibility of their salvation being centered in his person, and of the legal unity of the head and members, the Chinese understand the scheme as having its foundation in law and its superstructure in equity.

Christ, the Sacrifice.

"The idea of expiation is found in the earlier and later history of China." It is a solemn event when the Emperor, the vicegerent of heaven, the high-priest of the nation, in his vicarious character decends from his throne, robes himself in sack-cloth, makes public confession, becomes the substitute for his people and appears as the sin-bearer. During seven years of famine, B. C. 1766, the Emperor Tang "fasted, cut off his hair and nails, and in a plain cart drawn by white horses, clad in rushes, the guise of a sacrificial victim, he proceeded to a forest of mulberry trees and there prayed." He said, "When guilt is found anywhere in you who occupy the myriad regions, let it rest on me, the One Man. When guilt is found in me, the One Man, it shall not attach to you." Thirty-six centuries after, July 24, 1832, in the time of severe drought, the Emperor Taokwang offered the following prayer: "Oh! alas! Imperial Heaven! . . . this year the drought is most unusual. Summer is past, and no rain has fallen. . . . I, the minister of heaven, am placed over mankind, and am responsible for keeping the world in order and for tranquilizing the people. . . . I examine myself and consider my errors, looking up and hoping that I may obtain pardon. . . . Prostrate I beg Imperial Heaven to pardon my ignorance and stupidity, and to grant me self-renovation, for myriads of people are involved by me, the One Man."

There was a noted case in this city when the Literary Chancellor, who was condemned for selling degrees, was spared because his son took the father's place at the execution ground and lost his head. Often in country riots and insurrections where blood has been shed, one man, whose family has been liberally provided for by the survivors, steps forward, announces himself as the manslayer, and receives capital punishment. There is no difficulty in getting a heathen audience to understand the account of Christ's sufferings as given by Isaiah in the fifty-third chapter of his prophecies. As the beloved disciple wrote, "And he is the propitiation for our sins: and not for ours only, but also for the sins of the whole world." From this topic it is easy to pass to

Christ's Humanity

as a suitable subject on which to address a heathen

audience. That God is a Spirit, the great eternal I Am, is too infinite a thought for poor worms of the dust. The pagan seeks communion with beings in bodily shape, not far removed from his mortal sphere, who can understand his necessities. Thus Buddhism, with her myriads of gods, appeals to the feebleness of man. How completely the Man of Judea is adapted to the wants of the Jew and Gentile. He is "in the likeness of sinful flesh.' "And the word was made flesh and dwelt among us." "No man hath seen God at any time; the only begotten Son, which is in the bosom of the Father, he hath declared him." Come to Jesus. He was born a babe, grew in childhood years, walked on earth, talked with men, worked in his shop, ate, slept and was weary, held intercourse with friends, was joyous, was sorrowful, he lived, he died and was buried, and we, like him, shall rise again. "Wherefore it behooved him to be made like unto his brethren." Is man tempted? "For in that he himself hath suffered, being tempted, he is able to succor them that are tempted." Is he in want of sympathy? "For we have not an high priest which cannot be touched with the feeling of our infirmities." Is he unlettered? "Who can have compassion on the ignorant, and on them that are out of the way." Does he wish to pray? "Let us, therefore, come boldly unto the throne of grace." Jesus was the Son of Man.

The Divinity of Our Lord.

The Chinese are willing to acknowledge Jesus as the great sage of the west, the peer of Confucius, but to recognize Jesus the Saviour and Confucius the teacher, Jesus the Lord and Confucius the subject, Jesus the creator and Confucius the creature, Jesus as divine and Confucius as human, is a doctrine they utterly repudiate. It is just here that Christianity and Confucianism stand at the opposite poles. One of the four subjects upon which Confucius said he did not discourse was concerning the gods. He knew nothing about religion and believed less, so he taught nothing. Jesus came to teach divinity; he declared that he himself was God. This is the battle-field, and here the soldiers of Christ must expect a bloody conflict.

Simon Peter was the first to declare fully and forcibly this fundamental doctrine when he said to his Lord, "Thou art the Christ, the Son of the living God." Jesus said upon this confession (*petra*) he would build his church. From the way the Master spoke to his disciple we may infer that this is a very practical tenet of theology: "Blessed art thou, Simon Barjona, for flesh and blood hath not revealed it unto thee, but my Father which is in heaven." It is necessary to salvation that men accept Jesus as divine, for he himself says: "If ye believe not that I am he, ye shall die in your sins." As we go forth among the heathen we can proclaim this truth as the door to fellowship with God's people. When the eunuch confessed, "I believe that Jesus Christ is the Son of God," he was immediately baptized.

In this brief section we will not consider the testimony of the four evangelists which fill the pages of the Gospels, nor the glorious pæans of the Pauline epistles. The miracles of Christ as witnesses for his divinity, and the transcendent testimony of his resurrection from the dead as when he said, "I lay down my life that I might take it again. . . . I have power to lay it down and I have power to take it again," will not be mentioned. Only one witness is presented, and that is Christ himself.

To all the attributes of God he lays a personal claim. Is God eternal? Jesus said, "Before Abraham was, I am," using the self-existent title by which Jehovah announced himself on the Mount of God. Is God omnipresent? Christ said, "Where two or three are gathered together in my name, there am I in the midst of them." Is God omnipotent? "All power is given unto me in heaven and in earth," says the Master. Is God omniscient? "As the Father knoweth me, even so know I the Father," thus laying claim to a knowledge of the infinite. He says, "I and my Father are one." He reveals God to men. How expressive are the pronouns in these words of our Jesus: "If a man love me he will keep my words, and my Father will love him, and we will come unto him and make our abode with him."

He speaks of himself as the light of the world, the shepherd of a countless flock, the vine from which the branches obtain nourishment, the way, truth and life, the door of heaven, the living bread, the water of life, the resurrection and the life. He was before Abraham; of him Moses wrote, and David called him Lord. He was greater than Solomon and the temple, and declared himself Lord of the Sabbath. He requires faith and love and obedience, and while upon earth was the constant object of worship. His invitations were to *all* the weary and heavy laden; to the widow, the orphan, the tempted, the persecuted and the sin-burdened to come to him and find rest. He is the mediator in prayer, has ability to forgive sin, and is the architect of heaven. His dying testimony at Pilate's tribunal was to his divinity. Jesus is the resurrection. It was a stupendous act of power to restore Lazarus to life, but the same voice is to be heard by millions upon millions who sleep in their graves. He is to judge all men, all actions, all words, all thoughts, and to impartially bestow rewards. He foretells his glory when men "shall see heaven open and the angels of God ascending and descending upon the Son of man." The questions, then, that the missionary is to press upon the heart and conscience of a heathen congregation are, "What think ye of Christ?" "Whom say ye that I am?" When we behold the calmness of his assertions when he offers to forgive sin, renew the heart, save from sin and hell and bestow immortality and eternal life, we may exclaim, *Christus, si non Deus, non bonus.*

The minister must also preach Christ as

The Magnet of the Church.

Jesus said, "And I, if I be lifted up from the earth, will draw all men unto me." This he said signifying what death he should die, and foretelling the power of the cross to attract the nations. The apostle, in his message to the Gentiles, said, "We preach Christ crucified"; that is, in proclaiming the gospel he gave prominence to the doctrine of the blood. "Christ died for the ungodly," "it is Christ that died," "Jesus died." This was the foundation of the whole scheme of salvation. Let one note how often "cross," "blood," "sacrifice," "offering," "satisfaction," "propitiation," "priesthood," "lamb," "Redeemer," "salvation," and kindred words are used in reference to the death of Christ. Paul went further and declared, "God forbid that I should glory save in the cross of our Lord Jesus Christ." It was his chief joy and honor to tell of the cross, and so with all the messengers of salvation, as they go to the remotest ends of the earth. All the attributes of Jesus circle round the cross. His name pointed to Calvary, and there did he save his people from their sins. Was Christ meek and lowly in heart? "He was oppressed, and he was afflicted, yet he opened not his mouth: he is brought as a lamb to the slaughter, and as a sheep before her shearers is dumb, so he openeth not his mouth." Did he impress upon his disciples the duty of forgiving enemies? But what were his words compared with his example, as he hung upon the tree, "Father, forgive them; they know not what they do!" Was he subject to his parents in his youth? On the cross, when in the agony of a cruel death he made provision for his mother, there was a triumphant manifestation of filial duty. Did Christ say, "The Son of man is come to seek and save the lost"? What greater proof that when he bade the robber accompany him to Paradise! Did he love his own and love them to the end? "The good Shepherd giveth his life for the sheep." If one preaches Christ, he must of necessity preach the cross.

All the attributes of Jehovah are beautifully harmonized in the cross of our Redeemer: "Mercy and truth are met together; righteousness and peace have kissed each other. Truth shall spring out of the earth, and righteousness shall look down from heaven." Justice claimed the sinner's death; mercy pleaded for his life. The truth of Jehovah demanded the punishment of the guilty; love offered a substitute in his room and stead. Hatred of sin and affection for the sinner were both wondrously displayed.

There is no place in sacred story where the prophets so unite in a grand chorus as at the cross, and even the heathen may understand how holy men of old told of the death of the Son of God. The Saviour, whose sufferings with the eye of prescience they beheld, now hung upon the tree. His ancestor, the great King of Israel, there tuned his harp, and the evangelical prophet, who so eloquently preached of the dying Messiah, now knew how accurate was his description.

Gethsemane, with its "bloody sweat," and the mocking, scourging, and crowning with thorns at Pilate's tribunal, are scenes which impress a Chinese audience. The high priestly office in the solemn temple services may be distinctly set forth as prefiguring the great High Priest who was to make atonement for the sins of his people. The quickness of a Chinese execution, when the head is severed from the neck with one stroke of the knife, places in contrast the lingering, torturing death by crucifixion. No wonder the apostle wrote to the Gentiles about the "accursed death of the cross." He could say, "Christ hath redeemed us from the curse of the law, being made a curse for us; for it is written, Cursed is every one that hangeth on a tree."

The bloodless character of Buddhism, with its horror of animal sacrifices and its scheme of salvation by meritorious deeds, stands in contrast with the cross. With them it is "every man his own Saviour," and they know not the righteousness of another imputed to them and received by faith alone. The peoples of the earth must have looked upon Judea as a bloody nation. The daily sacrifices, the multitude of victims offered on the day of atonement, and the great occasions, as when King Solomon "offered a sacrifice of peace-offerings, which he offered unto the Lord, two and twenty thousand oxen and an hundred and twenty thousand sheep," and blood ran down the sides of Mount Moriah, must have impressed all who beheld the august worship. In the cross all the types and shadows of the ceremonial law were fulfilled. By one sacrifice never to be repeated Christ made an all-sufficient atonement for the sins of his people. "But now once in the end of the world hath he appeared to put away sin by the sacrifice of himself. And as it is appointed unto men once to die, but after this the judgment, so Christ was once offered to bear the sins of many." In this *oneness* that the sacred writer insists upon Christianity is totally unlike Confucianism. Offerings are made to their ancestors at every feast, and in the 1,500 "Temples of Literature," at the spring and autumn sacrifices 135,000 animals—bulls, sheep, and hogs—are placed before the tablets of Confucius and his company of wise men, besides the animals offered in sacrifice to the gods of war, of literature, of the wind, sun, stars, etc. The stream so pure and clear which flowed from the foot of Ararat has been diverted into the channels of literature, and the muddy currents bring devastation to the religious aspirations of the nation. "For the law . . . can never with those sacrifices which they offered year by year make the comers thereunto perfect." The Confucian sacrifices are powerless to effect a moral reformation. The Chinese, as a nation, have not yet learned that the shedding of blood must cease. "Christ was once offered."

The Gentiles are to be taught the infinite value of Jesus' blood, "the precious blood"; or, as Paul charged the Ephesian elders, "Feed the church of God, which he hath purchased with his own blood." They are to be told that "Without shedding of blood there is no remission"; and that "The blood of Jesus Christ cleanseth from all sin." It is Jesus, "the Lamb slain before the foundation of the world," the Lamb of God upon Calvary, and "the Lamb that was slain," but now in heaven is worthy "to receive power, and riches, and wisdom, and strength, and glory, and blessing," of whom we speak.

Above all, preaching the cross proves to the Gentiles the amazing love of God to sinful man. "God *so* loved the world, that he sent his only begotten son." "He that spared not his own Son, but delivered him up for us all, how shall he not with him also give us all things?" "In this was manifested the love of God toward us, because that God sent his only begotten Son into the world, that we might live through him. Herein is love, not that we loved God, but that he loved us, and sent his Son to be the propitiation for our sins." This is the strongest appeal that can be made to the children of men. If men at Calvary resist the offer of divine mercy, there is no further room for appeal. The picture of the Redeemer's sufferings does draw the nations, and the preaching of *Christ crucified* is made "the power of God and the wisdom of God," to the salvation of the Gentiles.

CHAPTER XIII.

Jesus, the Model Preacher to the Heathen.

SEVENTEEN hundred years before the coming of our Lord, his ancestor, Jacob, said, "Unto him shall the gathering of the people be." The evangelists say, "And Jesus went into all Galilee, teaching in their synagogues, and preaching the gospel of the kingdom . . . and his fame went throughout all Syria. . . . And there followed him great multitudes of people from Galilee, and from Decapolis (*i. e.*, the ten cities), and from Jerusalem, and from Judea, and from beyond Jordan." "And they came to him from every quarter." And why came they? It was to hear the prophet of Nazareth preach, "and all bare him witness, and wondered at the gracious words which proceeded out of his mouth." His disciples said to him, "Thou hast the words of eternal life." Grace was poured into his lips. As Jesus taught in the temple a band of officers was despatched by the Pharisees and the chief priests to take him. They stopped on the borders of the vast assembly, and heard Jesus cry, his clarion notes ringing throughout the sacred portals, "If any man thirst let him come unto me and drink." Directly the officers returned to the Sanhedrim sitting in their council of state, they demanded, "Why have ye not brought him?" The answer was, "Never man spake like this man."

Never did orator in Athens or Rome, London or Washington, equal the Man of Galilee in holding spell-bound, from early morn till dewy eve, the thousands who waited on his ministry. His voice, so clear, so majestic, and so sweet, could be heard throughout the vast concourse, high above the wind in the trees on the mountain-side, or the dashing of the breakers on the seashore; and the wilderness and the solitary place rejoiced because of the words of wisdom, power, truth, and love. The eloquence of Jesus is a theme worthy of classic hall and sacred tabernacle, and demands the special attention of the heralds of the cross in distant lands. Judea had been asleep for centuries amidst the splendors of the temple ritual, the doctors expounding the bare letter of the law—Oh, so cold and cheerless!—much as the Confucianists lecture in the temples on morality, when suddenly a great teacher arose, and awoke the slumbering people of God as he unfolded the spiritual life of the kingdom of righteousness; and no journey was too long, or road too rough, that their ears might once hear the joyful notes of salvation from his lips. Before Jesus commanded his disciples, "Go, preach," he set before them the perfect model of *missionary* preaching, or the evangelization of the multitudes, while to his apostles was assigned in part the work of *ministerial* preaching, or building up the church in faith and knowledge.

The life of our Saviour on earth was essentially a teaching ministry. He wrought great miracles, but it is a matter of surprise how little time these occupied. In "the twinkling of an eye" the divine power would flash forth, and wonders of love and mercy would be accomplished. Of an hour's work it is recorded: "And at even, when the sun did set, they brought unto him all that were diseased, and them that were possessed with devils. And all the city was gathered together at the door. And he healed many that were sick of divers diseases, and cast out many devils." Probably only a limited portion of the three years was taken up exclusively in miracles; for, as he healed the sick and raised the dead, he taught his disciples, and preached to the multitudes. He instructed his followers, answered questions, engaged in disputations, explained doubts, revealed the thoughts of his hearers, taught the people and preached as he journeyed, or wherever men might come, in the synagogues, in the wilderness, on the mountains, and beside the sea. The upper classes of the Jews—the high-priestly families, the doctors of the law, the scribes, Pharisees, and Sadducees—possessing the learning of the sacred books, had by degrees become the aristocracy of the nation; but when our Lord appeared, he broke down this caste, and pronounced it one of the proofs of his divine mission, that "the poor have the gospel preached to them."

How suited the teachings of Jesus to the minds of heathen audiences! While much that prophets and apostles wrote is too deep for the elementary instruction of an idolatrous people, the words of Christ, at once so profound and so simple; so easy to be understood, yet with such far-reaching depths, are perfectly adapted to a heathen congregation, so that expository discourses on the Gospels may be perfectly understood by the untutored pagan. A few of the discourses of our Lord, as the sermons on the mount and at the last supper, are recorded, but generally they are only the fragments of his sermons. No doubt the Master, like all missionaries to the people of Asia, often repeated the great truths he wished to impress upon the minds of men, weaving the same lessons together into the garments of salvation, as suited the various times and circumstances. It seems thus, that a harmony of the Gospels, except in an approximate degree, is an impossibility.

Wonderful is the testimony about Christ: "And without a parable spake he not unto them." "Behold," says the Master, as he drew pictures which for nineteen centuries have been admired by all nations and people. He awakened thought by his suggestive parables. There was not a formal division of the subject under a succession of heads, but a series of stereoscopic views, by the combination of which we have a complete survey of the whole. Taking no text, he found his text in the conditions of men—the rich man, the beggar, the judge, the widow, the merchant, the farmer—or took for his subject nature in her ever varying aspects—the fields and vineyards, the trees and flowers, the birds and fish—or selected his topic from the passing events of his ministry—the young man, the children, the blind, the lost.

In these parables the Master of assemblies grasped the leading truths which he wished to impress upon his disciples. What an array of glorious doctrines in the thirteenth chapter of Matthew: The sower and the seed, and his varied success; the devil with his tares, and his utter ruin; the mustard seed and the leaven, to prefigure the growth of the kingdom; the hid treasure and the pearls, to tell how precious the gospel is; and the separation of the fish, as a type of the coming judgment! These were not loosely thrown together, for at the close of the discourse the Master said, "Therefore, every scribe which is instructed unto the kingdom of heaven is like unto a man that is an householder, which bringeth forth out of his treasures things new and old." In what book of sermons do we find such a single logical train of thought as in the three parables of the lost—the lost sheep, the lost money, the lost son; the earnestness in seeking, the longing to find, the rejoicings in both the earthly and the heavenly homes? Or take the discourse on the shepherd and the sheep, and what a multitude of thoughts the preacher groups around his text! So wondrous are his words, that it requires patient study, holy meditation, earnest prayer, and the enlightening power of the Holy Ghost to enable one to appreciate their beauty and sublimity.

The teaching of Jesus illustrates the progressive method of instruction. He, the great Fisher of men, as anxious to catch a single fish as a great multitude, sat beside Jacob's well, when a poor woman appeared as an auditor. He could have stated at once that he was the hope of Israel; but, hinting at his divine power, he simply asked for a cup of cold water. The woman, in her second reply, began, like the Chinese, to talk about her ancestors; but the Saviour answered by preaching on one of the most profound doctrines of inspiration, the water of life. When she, like the friends to whom we come, asked for temporal benefits, he did not upbraid her for her stupidity, but dealt tenderly with her weakness. He startled her with the conviction of sin, revealing her character in all its awful deformity. "Sir, I perceive that thou art a prophet," was her reply; but she immediately turned the subject on sacred mountains, while Jesus showed her that, though "salvation was of the Jews," that God, who is a Spirit, seeketh for true worshippers who shall worship him in spirit and in truth. Such preaching stirred up thoughts of the coming of Messias; and when the Master said unto her, "I that speak unto thee am he," she, the first messenger to the heathen, went her way, and said, "Is not this the Christ?" Thus was our Lord the model practical teacher in commencing a most spiritual discourse in a most natural way, and rising from physical wants to the necessities of the soul.

A marked characteristic of the ministry of the Son of man was that "The common people heard him gladly." Not so with Confucius, whose followers were the *literati*. To preach to a company of intelligent hearers, accustomed to read and to think, is comparatively an easy task, but to reach the multitude a speaker must be both perspicuous and attractive. Jesus knew how to touch the springs of the mind and heart. Among the most precious recorded discourses of our Lord are those he delivered at the tables of the rich, when feasts were specially given in his honor. The company reclining on their couches hung on the lips of him who gave them meat to eat which they knew not of. His methods of interrogation were very suggestive, as when he said unto the man who was blind, but now saw, "Dost thou believe on the Son of God?" The natural reply of an inquirer was, "Who is he, Lord, that I might believe on him?"

The Master constantly preached doctrine. He presented to his disciples a glorious array of the fundamental doctrines of Scripture, and connected all these heavenly truths with himself, thus making them fresh and attractive. Throughout he appears as the living, loving, dying, rising, descending Christ. His teaching is most impressive in that he weaves the warp of doctrine and the woof of practice into the garment of a holy Christian life.

The pathos of Christ's teaching melted the hearts

of his hearers. He sounded the key-note of his mission, when he sat on the Mount, and his disciples came unto him, and his lips pronounced, "Blessed." Wondrous are the objects of these blessings and the fruition bestowed on each. His themes were, for the most part, of the gentler kind, and appealed to the tenderest emotions of human nature. It had been foretold, "He shall not cry, nor lift up nor cause his voice to be heard in the streets. A bruised reed shall he not break, and the smoking flax shall he not quench." He declared what his ministry was in the passage he selected in the pulpit of Nazareth: "The Spirit of the Lord is upon me because he hath anointed me to preach the gospel to the poor; he hath sent me to heal the broken-hearted, to preach deliverance to the captives, and recovery of sight to the blind, to set at liberty them that are bruised, to preach the acceptable year of the Lord." The son of David set the example of a tender, loving style of preaching which proves what he said, "I am meek and lowly in heart."

He set before his people the Fatherhood of God. The chosen nation had known the God of Israel by the uncommunicable name of Jehovah, who "was glorious in holiness, fearful in praises, doing wonders." They delighted to reverence his majesty, and stand in awe before his awful throne. Christ taught "God is Love," and spoke to them of his Father, and taught his disciples to pray, "Our Father." It was a mighty step in the revelation when men were taught the filial spirit as they approached the Most High. In this land, where the promise of long life to those who honor their parents has been so signally fulfilled to the nation, the missionary can show that religion is simply filial piety extended towards the great Father of us all. The many and oft-repeated exhortations of their sacred books may illustrate the words of Scripture, "A son honoreth a father, . . if I then be a father, where is mine honor?" They have the five relations, the goverment, the filial, the conjugal, the fraternal and the friendly, as the five fingers, but they lack the religious or the relation between God and man, which, as the palm of the hand, is the centre from which all human relations diverge. May the Chinese soon learn of Christ, and say, "Now, O Lord, thou art our father."

Jesus also unfolded the Sinaic code, and thundered Sinai's anathemas against those who rebelled against the offers of mercy. When, in Matthew xxiii. 23, he cried repeatedly, "Woe unto you, scribes and Pharisees, hypocrites!" he denounced in fearful terms the consequences of an outward observance of the forms of worship, and at the same time a hidden opposition to the spirit of Christianity.

In his preaching he insisted on his credentials, that he came from the Father, and was sent by the Father. "I seek not mine own will, but the will of the Father which hath sent me." "He that receiveth me receiveth him that sent me." It was the lofty claims he made to divine honors that awoke the bitter opposition which led at last to his crucifixion.

At the very beginning of his ministry, he declared, "The kingdom of heaven is at hand." How startling the announcement! They mistook it for the kingdom of Israel; but he came to establish the kingdom of heaven on this earth, just as he taught men to pray, "Thy kingdom come," and sent out his disciples to establish the kingdom among the nations. They were not to say, "Who shall ascend into heaven?" for he declared, "The kingdom of God is at hand; repent ye, and believe the gospel." He continued the message of his forerunner, "the voice in the wilderness," and preached "repentance unto God." In every form of expression he insisted upon faith as the fundamental doctrine of the society that he established:

"Have faith in God." "Ye believe in God, believe also in me." Before a miracle was performed, he required a living faith in the recipient of his blessing. "That whosoever believeth on him should not perish. . . . He that believeth on him is not condemned; but he that believeth not is condemned already, because he hath not believed in the name of the only begotten Son of God."

There is no point on which Christianity and Confucianism are more divergent than on the treatment of enemies, and there is no place where it is more important to insist upon the doctrine of forgiveness than in China. How appropriate the words of Jesus, "Ye have heard that it hath been said, Thou shalt love thy neighbor, and hate thine enemy; but I say unto you, Love your enemies, bless them that curse you, do good to them that hate you, and pray for them which despitefully use you and persecute you; that ye may be the children of your Father which is in heaven."

When our Master called his disciples, ordained them to be with him, commissioned them, and sent them forth, he placed before them in distinct terms how they must endure hardness as good soldiers of Jesus Christ. Missionaries in this land, in view of the many local and general persecutions which overtake native converts, must repeat what Jesus said to those about to bear his yoke: "And ye shall be brought before governors and kings for my sake, for a testimony against them and the Gentiles. . . . And the brother shall deliver up the brother to death, and the father, the child. . . . And ye shall be hated of all men for my name's sake." It is not an easy thing for a man to be a Christian in China. Petty troubles from family divisions, from refusing to join in the worship of ancestors, and for declining to contribute to idol processions and worship, arise on every hand.

The messenger of salvation stands appalled before the gigantic array of idolatry and superstition. The promise of Christ comes a solace to his heart, and there is scarcely a text more appreciated by the native Christian than, "Ye shall know the truth, and the truth shall make you free." We fight not the darkness, we turn on the light. "The truth as it is in Jesus," taught to believers, sets them free from the chains of sin and Satan. "God hath from the beginning chosen them to salvation through sanctification of the Spirit and belief of the truth." They obey the truth, and walk in the truth.

There is no class to whom the gospel comes more with the rainbow of promise than to the women of China. Did Jesus love Mary and Martha? Did Mary Magdalene, and Joanna, the wife of Chuza, Herod's steward, and Susanna, and many others, minister unto him of their substance? Was there a group of women standing beside the cross, witnessing his accursed death? As soon as the holy Sabbath was passed, did they repair to the sepulchre? And what religion on earth, save Christianity, says, "Suffer little children to come unto me," and "Out of the mouths of babes and sucklings thou hast perfected praise"?

The philosophers of the Middle Kingdom treat of political economy, ethics, and filial piety; our Lord and Master, of eternal themes. The value of the soul is a theme he treats as of transcendent importance. The good young man, the rich fool, and Dives being in Hades in torment, illustrated the folly of setting the affections upon the things of earth, and neglecting the soul. He sets before this class the problem of profit and loss, and then asks, "And what shall a man give in exchange for his soul?" In this land, by the doctrines of the divisibility of the soul and its frequent transmigrations, men lose sight of its importance, and let the subject lapse into utter forgetfulness. The value of the soul, and its future of happiness or woe, is the missionary's great theme.

How the Chinese, like the Jews, love to "lay up treasure on earth"! How their robes of silk, satin, and fur are ruined by the rainy and mouldy season! And how high the walls must be, and the gates so strongly barred, to keep out the thieves! And the poverty! poverty!! As the millions scarcely exist, how much "anxious thought" for the bare food necessary "to keep soul and body together"! How appropriate to troubled hearts are the words, "Therefore, take no thought, saying, What shall we eat? or, What shall we drink? or, Wherewithal shall we be clothed? (For after all these things do the Gentiles seek); for your heavenly Father knoweth ye have need of all these things."

The most impressive feature of Chinese civilization that strikes the new arrival is the number of burden-bearers. Men are beasts of burden. Horses are not used on the well-watered plains of China, because the food must be garnered to sustain the life of man. They may hear the voice of the Son of man, "Come unto me, all ye that are weary and heavy-laden, and I will give you rest." How precious the invitations of Jesus! How the Chinaman, in this land of feasts, can understand the parables of the wedding feast and of the great supper!

The teachings of Jesus were eminently practical! He did not give men the theory of prayer, but simply told them, "Ask, and ye shall receive." He did not try to prove what he affirmed, but, instead, made a personal application of the truth to the hearts of the objectors, as when in regard to works of mercy on the Sabbath he inquired, "How much then is a man better than a sheep?" In China the Mandarins are given office away from home, in a distant province, just as kingdoms were distributed in the Roman empire. How forcible, then, are Christ's oft-repeated teachings about his future coming: "A certain nobleman went into a far country to receive for himself a kingdom, and to return." Alas! how many say in their heart, "My lord delayeth his coming."

The above is but a faint outline of the way Jesus taught, a few shells picked up from the shore of the gospel ocean. Jesus is our pattern and our guide, but nowhere more so than in preaching to the Gentiles. Let the missionary of the cross catch the spirit of Christ, emulate his example, explain his words, and strive to preach as the Master preached. The extraordinary gift of miracles does not pertain to this dispensation, but the ordinary gift of preaching is the glory of the present age.

In preaching the mind and words of Jesus we have an entirely new field in China. There is little in Confucianism or Buddhism to furnish texts or subjects or illustrations for public speaking, but the Bible affords an illimitable supply. There is a glory about the pulpit with its thousands and tens of thousands of mighty orators, who have striven to hold up before the people the pictures of religion Jesus bequeathed to mankind. Following in his footsteps there is an exceeding great army who stand upon Mount Zion, and bring the message of great joy to all people. We are to seek in our preaching that there may be wider, fuller, and richer provision; that in the language of the Good Shepherd the sheep " shall go in and out and find pasture." "Follow me," says Jesus as he preached the gospel of the kingdom, and the future of the pulpit in Sinim depends on how closely the disciples imitate their great Exemplar.

CHAPTER XIV.

Paul, the Preacher.

THE missionary in heathen lands constantly studies the life and character of the great apostle to the Gentiles, who was the first exponent of evangelistic theology. The Divinity Hall which he attended was the same as that where Moses received his long training, the sandy plain of Arabia. The "eleven" listened to the Master while he spake to them on earth; Paul, to the voice from the excellent glory. His three years' curriculum left an indelible impression upon his mind. Writes he: "I will come to visions and revelations of the Lord. I knew a man in Christ above fourteen years ago. . . How that he was caught up into Paradise and heard unspeakable words, which it is not lawful for a man to utter." Things of earth faded from view after he beheld the great multitude, which no man could number, of all nations, and kindreds, and people, and tongues, which stood before the throne and before the Lamb. No wonder that ever afterwards he was "willing rather to be absent from the body and to be present with the Lord." He could exclaim, "For me to live is Christ." "I am crucified with Christ; nevertheless I live; yet not I but Christ liveth in me: and the life which I now live in the flesh I live by the faith of the Son of God, who loved me and gave himself for me."

Paul did not, however, sit and dream of heaven, his aim was that he might finish his course with joy, and the ministry which he had received of the Lord Jesus. He asserts and repeats his assertion, "I am ordained a preacher, and an apostle, a teacher of the Gentiles." "That I should be the minister of Jesus Christ to the Gentiles." The Lord said, "He is a chosen vessel unto me, to bear my name before the Gentiles." His motto was, "Inasmuch as I am the apostle to the Gentiles, I magnify my office, and in his humility he could exclaim, "Unto me, who am less than the least of all saints, is this grace given, that I should preach amongst the Gentiles the unsearchable riches of Christ."

No mere man has ever lived who made such a sensation by preaching as Paul did. His first question: Is Jehovah "the God of the Jews only? Is he not also of the Gentiles? Yes, of the Gentiles also," astonished the nations, for the Romans spoke to the Jews of "*Your* Jehovah," just as the

Chinese do to us of "*Your* Jesus." The gifted preacher went from land to land, and all heard him speak in their own tongues the wonderful works of God. The philosophers of Greece invited him to the Areopagus to speak before assembled Athens, for said they, "Thou bringest certain strange things to our ears." Demetrius declared, "Moreover ye see and hear, that not alone at Ephesus, but almost throughout all Asia, this Paul hath persuaded and turned away much people, saying that they be no gods which are made with hands." At Thessalonica the unbelieving Jews drew Paul's host before the rulers, crying, "These that have turned the world upside down have come hither also."

Among the gifts bestowed so abundantly upon him was that of the eloquent tongue. We have only epitomes of his great discourses left us, but they have served as models for pulpit orators since the Christian era. The grace with which he introduced himself to the audience, the adaptability of his speech, the hanging his theme on some felicitous circumstance, the pointed use of appropriate quotations, his masterly tact in presenting his arguments, the logic of his reasoning, the cogency of his appeals, the soul-earnestness of his manner, and, more than all, the transcendent claims of the truths he proclaimed, placed him in the rank above Cicero and Demosthenes. With his companion, Barnabas, he came to Iconium, and went into the synagogue, and they "so spake that a great multitude, both of the Jews and also of the Greeks, believed." The historian uses the simple description "so spake." A great ingathering was the result.

Paul was an itinerant, and, with Jerusalem as a focus, he made his three great missionary journeys. He loved the Holy City, and, whether to attend the feast, or to bear alms to the believing poor, thither he was bound in the Spirit. From city to city, and from country to country, in journeys by land and by sea, he went, proclaiming salvation; sometimes remaining three weeks; again, three months; perhaps a year and a half, or at other places, two or three years. It was by these labors, scattered over Europe and Asia Minor, that he was enabled to plant the gospel in so many places. "Thrice I suffered shipwreck, a night and a day I have been in the deep; in journeyings often, in perils of waters, in perils of robbers, in perils by mine own countrymen, in perils by the heathen, in perils in the city, in perils in the wilderness, in perils in the sea, in perils among false brethren; in weariness and painfulness, in watchings often, in hunger and thirst, in fastings often, in cold and nakedness."

At Corinth, rather than suffer the reproach of "eating the church's rice" by remaining in a wealthy city instead of preaching to the poor in the country, he abode with Priscilla and Aquila, and wrought, "because he was of the same craft." He could point to his broad and hard hands, which had toiled at the coarse tent-cloth, and say to the elders, "Yea, ye yourselves know that these hands have ministered unto my necessities, and to them that were with me." With what a touch of sarcasm he could write, "For what is it wherein ye were inferior to other churches, except it be that I myself was not burdensome to you? *Forgive me this wrong.*"

The apostle was his own forerunner. The disciples were gathered at Jerusalem, to the number of many thousands, and probably of tens of thousands, and spending their time in receiving the gifts of the Holy Spirit, and enjoying Christian fellowship and community of goods, when suddenly Saul of Tarsus made great havoc among them, haling men and women, and committing them to prison; and thus scattered abroad, they dwelt in all the cities of the Roman Empire. In after years they, forgetting the things that were passed, were ready to welcome the former blasphemer and persecutor, and opened their houses for preaching. During the centuries preceding the Christian era, the Jews, afraid to dwell in Palestine, and being, like the Chinese, men of commercial enterprise, spread themselves throughout the adjacent countries, and by their wealth commanded great influence. They remembered the God of Abraham, and built houses of worship. In these Paul was privileged to hold divine service, and to reason with those who objected to his teachings. The missionaries of the present day have no such advantages.

Often he stood face to face with heathenism, with no pious Jew or humble Christian to aid him in his work. What a picture he gives of the condition and state of the Gentile world! It was a faithful description of the city sitting upon seven hills, and of the nations dwelling on the plains, a portrait which for accuracy in detail and faithfulness in delineation has never been equaled; so he knew what was before him. When he concludes, "There is none righteous, no, not one; there is none that understandeth, there is none that seeketh after God. They are all gone out of the way, they are together become unprofitable; there is none that doeth good, no, not one," it is to pave the way for preaching justification by faith in the blood of Jesus Christ, and the impartation of his righteousness.

The signs and wonders which Paul wrought made a powerful impression upon the apostolic church. At Lystra, the cripple, "impotent in his feet," but potent in his faith, hobbled to preaching; and the man of God shouted. "Stand upright upon thy feet," and so surprised was the crowd, that they "lifted up their voices, saying, The gods are come down to us in the likeness of men." The news spread rapidly, and the populace flocked to the campus. The preacher, seeing his audience rapidly increasing, and listening with awe and reverence, warmed in his theme, and his ringing voice was heard by the great assembly, when, lo! a company of priests, with sacrificial oxen and floral crowns, appeared. Worship was to be offered to these divine beings. Nothing could restrain the assembly till, with garments rent in twain, they rushed amidst the worshippers and cried, "Sirs, why do ye these things? We also are men of like passions with you, and preach unto you that ye should turn from these vanities unto the living God." He then delivered a brief discourse on natural theology, showing that an abundant harvest is a proof of the existence of

God. "He left not himself without witness, in that he did good, and gave us rain from heaven, and fruitful seasons, filling our hearts with food and gladness."

The apostle was not an independent evangelist, going when and where he chose, but his labors were directed by a power above! He wished to preach in Asia; he was "forbidden of the Holy Ghost." He then "assayed to go into Bythinia, but the Spirit suffered him not." There was work for him at another place, but he knew not where. When he came to Troy it was revealed to him in a night vision. On the opposite shore there stood a man "and prayed him, saying, Come over into Macedonia and help us." What a series of events followed this special call: The pious women by the river-side, the open heart of Lydia, the little soothsayer, the arrest, the scourging, the songs in the night, the conversion of the jailer, and the sermon,—perhaps the simplest exposition of the plan of salvation to be found in the Bible.

From Philippi he went to Thessalonica. This is one of the most remarkable passages in the life of Paul. The epistle to these Christians tells of the effect of his preaching: The number of converts, the power of the gospel, the full assurance of the believers, the reception of the message as the word of God, their becoming followers of the apostle, their joy in the Holy Ghost, the fame of their faith, the turning from dumb idols, and the constant expectation of the Lord's coming; and all this from three weeks' missionary labor!

Driven by persecution, he arrived at Athens, and there his spirit waxed hot against the superabounding idolatries. His preaching was unremitting, both in the churches and on the streets, and his labors reached their acme when he stood on Mars' Hill and preached the grandest missionary sermon, perhaps, ever delivered. It is one of the most familiar passages to the church, and one which has proved an inspiration to thousands of faithful ministers during all these centuries. These words will continue to ring throughout the nations till "the kingdoms of this world become the kingdoms of the Lord and of his Christ."

The Master to this servant verified his promise, "Lo! I am with you alway." At the great heathen city of Corinth the work seemed appalling in its magnitude. "Then spake the Lord to Paul in the night by a vision, Be not afraid, but speak, and hold not thy peace: for I am with thee, and no man shall set on thee to hurt thee: for I have much people in this city." This assurance has cheered many a weary toiler.

When his labors at Corinth were ended we have a proof at Ephesus how "mightily grew the word of God and prevailed." This city, like Soochow, was filled with hordes of astrologers, geomancers, magicians, diviners, soothsayers, exorcists, and all that class who plied their lucrative avocations in the temples, markets and public places. Paul preached and "wrought special miracles," "and fear fell on them all, and the name of the Lord Jesus was magnified. . . . Many of them also which used curious arts brought their books together, and burned them before all men: and they counted the price of them, and found it fifty thousand pieces of silver."

At Jerusalem, arrested on a false charge, he was brought before the council. "The night following the Lord stood by him, and said, Be of good cheer, Paul; for as thou hast testified of me in Jerusalem, so must thou bear witness also at Rome." Before this, at his conversion, it was said, "He is a chosen vessel unto me, to bear my name before the Gentiles and kings." He stood before Felix. He touched not on minor points of governmental policy or educational interests, but "reasoned of righteousness, temperance and judgment to come." The governor trembled. After two long years of imprisonment, Festus succeeded

Felix, and when King Agrippa came to Caesarea Paul was brought before him. It was a majestic assembly, for the king came "with great pomp and entered into the place of hearing, with the chief captains and principal men of the city." After a most graceful exordium, "I think myself happy, King Agrippa, because I shall answer for myself this day before thee," he based his defence on the facts of his conversion, his call to preach and the resurrection of our Lord. What an example to those who witness for Christ before rulers! Agrippa cried out, "Almost thou persuadest me to be a Christian." The aged prisoner, raising aloft his arms, bound with the felon's chain, exclaimed, "I would to God, that not only thou, but also all that hear me this day, were both almost, and altogether such as I am, except these bonds." No wonder this touching spectacle moved the king and the governor, and their judgment was, that were it not for his appeal he might be set at liberty.

His latter years, while under a guard of soldiers, were busily employed in speaking to the numbers who came to visit him and in writing letters, which are the means of the conversion of thousands and tens of thousands of the Gentiles. "Paul, the prisoner of the Lord," still preaches in three hundred tongues. The cords were drawn tighter and tighter around him, and from the cold vault of the Mamertine dungeon he could write in lines of light, "I am now ready to be offered, and the time of my departure is at hand. I have fought a good fight, I have finished my course, I have kept the faith; henceforth there is laid up for me a crown of righteousness, which the Lord, the righteous judge, shall give me at that day."

CHAPTER XV.

THE WORK OF THE HOLY SPIRIT.

WHEN the minister of the gospel goes to pagan lands he tries by research and inquiry to find out what basis there is for religious instruction, and what latent truths there are in the heathen mind upon which he may build his argument. In teaching theology there is the vast structure of the three religions supplying thought and language for teaching the true by the contrast with idolatry and superstition. When, however, the preacher begins to set forth the character of the third person of the Trinity there is absolutely nothing in natural religion to indicate his existence and work. It is purely a doctrine of revelation.

The importance to the Gentiles of the gift of the Holy Spirit cannot be overrated. The gift of tongues by which men began to speak in foreign languages was the first public manifestation of his presence in the church. The ordination at Antioch of the two first evangelists to the heathen was at the instance of the Holy Ghost, who said, "Separate me Barnabas and Saul for the work whereunto I have called them." "So they, being sent forth by the Holy Ghost, departed." Great ingatherings into the church followed the outpouring of the Spirit. While Peter was preaching, "the Holy Ghost fell on all them which heard the word. And they of the circumcision which believed were astonished . . . because that on the Gentiles also was poured out the gift of the Holy Ghost." The Book of Acts is not so much the acts of the apostles as the acts of the Holy Spirit, which he wrought through their instrumentality. As the great work of missions began with the procession of the Spirit and is continued by his presence and power, the person, character and glory of the Holy Ghost must be distinctly set before the church in a heathen land.

The Spirit is not to be preached simply as an influence or a breath, but as a distinct person, who is a sovereign, to whom prayer is to be offered and from whom blessings are to descend. His essential divinity must be insisted upon in distinct terms, and he be acknowledged as the third person in the adorable Trinity, co-equal with the Father and with the Son. The awful guards that have been placed around his sacred person and majesty may well make the sons of men fear to offend against him: "All manner of sin and blasphemy shall be forgiven unto men; but the blasphemy against the

Holy Ghost shall not be forgiven unto men. And whosoever speaketh a word against the Son of man, it shall be forgiven him; but whosoever speaketh against the Holy Ghost, it shall not be forgiven him, neither in this world, neither in the world to come." Men are to pray "to be filled with the Holy Ghost," but they are to realize the terrible nature of this petition, for he is the Spirit of judgment, and there is, as it were, a permanent judgment-day set up in the soul of man.

The Saviour promised that the Spirit should convince the world of sin. The heathen seek not God, because they do not feel that they are guilty at his bar, rebels who refuse his authority, and neglect to worship him who is their Lord and God. When the Spirit is poured out, then the heathen, who now "sit at ease," shall look upon him "whom they have pierced, and they shall mourn for him, as one mourneth for his only son." Then will they come to the "fountain opened to the house of David and to the inhabitants of Jerusalem for sin and for uncleanness," just as, on the day of Pentecost, the great congregation "were pricked in their heart."

He is to convince the world of righteousness: of the want of original righteousness, the vanity of human righteousness, and the inability of those "who, being ignorant of God's righteousness," go "about to establish their own righteousness." It is only the Holy Spirit which can lead a dying heathen to behold the beauty of the seamless robe of Christ's righteousness, the "wedding garment," in which arrayed he may be a welcome guest at the marriage supper of the Lamb.

The Spirit is to convince the world of judgment, and make men know that "God shall bring every work into judgment, with every secret thing, whether it be good, or whether it be evil." Natural religion gives many intimations of coming judgment, but these are written simply on the stone tablets of the temples, and are read "in the letter," without the thought of a personal judgment. The Spirit makes the fearful realities of the great day of final accounts to pass before the view of those who are hastening to this great tribunal.

The Holy Spirit will lead men to true repentance. The language of China is rich in its terms for repentance, and a volley of synonyms can be poured into the ears of an audience; yet they produce no effect, save the general admission that these things ought to be so. There is no topic where illustration is so easy, and which may be enforced with more power; yet, unless the Holy Spirit cements the word, the gospel architect laboreth but in vain.

The great hope of the Gentiles is in the regenerating power of the Spirit. The philosophers of China deal boldly with human nature, and their systems of ethics are studied in every school in the land. The "Three-character Classic," the first primer placed in the hands of a boy, begins, "Man's nature is originally good." Mencius speaks very beautifully of the "child's heart." In his discussions about man's nature, while acknowledging the existence of evil, he declares that men are naturally inclined to good. The people constantly talk of "the heart," and purity of motive is spoken of as "Buddha's heart." The essential goodness of human nature is a tenet in Chinese philosophy to which the high and the low, the learned and the unlearned, tenaciously cling. Men may preach against it as they will, they make no impression till the Spirit descends, and seals the truth on the conscience.

The Chinese need conversion. How touching the scene when "Jesus called a little child unto him, and set him in the midst of them, and said, Verily I say unto you, Except ye be converted, and become as little children, ye shall not enter into the kingdom of heaven." There is a glorious promise, "Then will I sprinkle clean water upon you, and ye shall be clean: from all your filthiness and from all your idols will I cleanse you. A new heart also will I give you, and a new spirit will I put within you: and I will take the stony heart out of your flesh, and I will give you an heart of flesh. And I will put my Spirit within you." It is for them to know in their personal experience, "If any man be in Christ, he is a new creature: old things are passed away; behold, all things are become new." The necessity of the new birth must be pressed upon them. "Verily, verily I say unto thee, Except a man be born of water and of the Spirit, he cannot enter into the kingdom of God. . . . Marvel not that I say unto thee, Ye must be born again." We rejoice in this dispensation of the Holy Spirit, and that he can produce this glorious change in the hearts of a mighty people. It is altogether beyond the resources of man, and is an act of sovereign, almighty power.

The messenger of salvation goes not forth in his own strength, for Jesus commanded his disciples, "Tarry ye in the city of Jerusalem until ye be endued with power from on high," and his last recorded words were, "Ye shall receive power, after that the Holy Ghost is come upon you." Many centuries before, the angel said to Jacob, "As a prince hast thou power with God and with man."

The promise, not of temporal, but of spiritual, power to those who should be witnesses for Christ unto the uttermost part of the earth is a wonderful factor in the evangelization of the nations. The words of the Master are true, for the Holy Ghost did come, and is now abiding with the church; and the minister must see to it that his own heart is prepared as an inn for the reception of the heavenly guest. Though the extraordinary gifts of miracles and tongues are not now given to the church, yet the ordinary and permanent gifts abound, and remain as its legacy. Among these may be mentioned persuasive eloquence, or the power of attracting men to the cross by the skilful use of reasoning, rhetoric, and elocution. There is a mighty power in the pulpit, and when men speak with the tongues of men and of angels, and at the same time have a burning desire to save souls, the Spirit of truth will guide the hearers to embrace the truth in the love of it. Another gift of the Spirit is the power of endurance amidst discouragements and difficulties, trials and perplexities. It is the "long patience" of which James speaks, the "perseverance of the saints." Another power is joy in the Holy Ghost, which joy gives vigor and elasticity to the laborer. It was said of the Master, "Who, for the joy that was set before him, endured the cross." Power in prayer is a gift of the Holy Ghost. "The effectual fervent prayer of a righteous man availeth much,"—even of men "subject to like passions as we are." The power of "rightly dividing the word of truth" is a special gift to those who "speak as the oracles of God."

The question comes, How then is this power to be obtained? Sometimes great gifts are bestowed suddenly upon the minister in holy things, but, as a general rule, the good soldier of Christ obtains his strength gradually by the use of the means given him. When Israel took possession of the promised land the heathen nations were not conquered in one decisive battle, they were put out "little by little" before the chosen people. It is thus "little by little" the promised power is obtained. The law of nature and grace here holds good. Just as the athlete obtains physical power by long and tedious preparation, so also the ripe fruits of the Christian life do not come to maturity in a day, but through a series of years, under the disciplining hand of divine Providence. We are to increase in power as well as to grow in grace. To be "wise unto salvation" in understanding the Scriptures is power; to have a tender compassion for dying men and an earnest desire to win souls is power; to be diligent in the sacred businesss of preaching the gospel is a power in convincing men of the truth of the message; and to pray without ceasing supplies one with a full suit of armor from the upper chamber in Jerusalem. The Holy Spirit takes the natural gifts, refines and developes them, and by his quickening influence makes these to be a power in the church. This power is not a permanent gift, for as food must be taken daily to obtain bodily strength, so this blessing of the Spirit must be sought hourly by communion with God. "Be thou faithful unto death, and I will give thee a crown of life," says Jesus. "To him that overcometh" are the seven promises given. The one great petition missionaries offer at a throne of divine grace is that the Holy Spirit may be poured out. The blessing on the preached word, the quickening of the dead bones on Asia's plains, the sanctification of the church, all comes from his divine power. He, the Sovereign Spirit, acts directly on the sinner's heart, and his influence does not pass through the minister to the object, so it is the power of the Holy Ghost, and not man's power, that brings men to the Saviour, yet he graciously uses men as instruments, and bestows his gifts upon them that they may lead others to embrace Jesus Christ, who is so freely offered in the gospel.

> O Spirit of the living God,
>   In all thy plenitude of grace,
> Where'er the foot of man hath trod,
>   Descend on our apostate race.
>
> Baptize the nations; far and nigh
>   The triumph of the cross record;
> The name of Jesus glorify,
>   Till every kindred call him Lord.

CHAPTER XVI.

THE WONDERS OF THE LAST DAYS.

THE Chinese views of religion are surprisingly materialistic. The missionary must not only teach the people their duties to God and their fellow-men; he must carry them beyond the confines of the grave to the great events which may be near at hand. One prominent topic must be

THE SECOND COMING OF OUR LORD.

Jesus taught the doctrine of the second coming so repeatedly that it becomes a prominent feature of the New Testament theology. "Watch, therefore, for ye know not what hour your Lord doth come." "Watch, therefore, for ye know neither the day nor the hour wherein the Son of man cometh." "And what I say unto you I say unto all, Watch." Just as ancient Israel's greatest hope was "when Messiah cometh," so the pole star of the Christian is "looking for that blessed hope and the glorious appearing of the great God and our Saviour Jesus Christ." As the apostles went among the heathen they bade them turn "to God from idols, to serve the living and true God, and to await for his Son from heaven."

Especially the disciples at Thessalonica continued in "the patient waiting for Christ," and this fact gave them great joy and rejoicing.

The Chinese often ask us, "Have you ever seen Jesus?" and we reply, "No; but these eyes shall behold him." "For I know that my Redeemer liveth, and that he shall stand at the latter day upon the earth." Preaching his second coming presents the living Jesus particularly and specially before the minds of men. The hearers look upon what is preached as a doctrine which is good, as a creed which may be accepted or rejected, or as a system with which they have no special concern. In presenting his future advent, we have the *living* Christ, "which was dead and is alive," the *reigning* Christ, "who hath on his vesture and on his thigh a name written, King of kings and Lord of lords," and the *personal* Christ, who will appear in our sight. The words of the Master, so oft repeated about the coming of the Son of man, must be oft repeated in the ears of the men of China.

The way he will come is easily understood. As the prophet at Babylon said, "I saw in the night visions, and, behold, one like the Son of man came with the clouds of heaven," so when on Olive's brow "a cloud received him out of the sight" of his adoring disciples, the two angelic messengers said, "This same Jesus, which is taken up from you into heaven, shall so come in like manner as ye have seen him go into heaven."

The quickness of his appearing Jesus himself describes, "As the lightning cometh out of the east and shineth even unto the west, so shall also the coming of the Son of man be." It will be preceded by a time of great wickedness, when "that wicked shall be revealed, whom the Lord shall consume with the Spirit of his mouth, and shall destroy with the brightness of his coming," a time of sin, even as the period preceding the flood, and like unto the days of the cities of the plain. Nothing could be more graphic than Christ's own words, "And then shall appear the sign of the Son of man in heaven: and then shall all the tribes of the earth mourn, and they shall see the Son of man coming in the clouds of heaven with power and great glory," "when he cometh in the glory of his Father with the holy angels." The missionary is to say to the heathen, "Jesus is coming! Prepare to meet thy God." The apostle could preach so tenderly, "If any man love not the Lord Jesus Christ, let him be anathema. The Lord cometh." To the pagan must be explained how joyful the hope that fills the heart of the believer in view of this glorious event.

The Resurrection.

In the fifteenth chapter of First Corinthians, the apostle treats of the resurrection of Christ and the resurrection of believers in the same passage. There is not a more enchanting picture to present to the heathen than the rising of our Lord from the dead. The night scene of the sepulchre in the rocky mount: the body laid carefully away, the heavy stone, the governor's seal, the military guard, the sad Sabbath; the morning scene: the earthquake, the stone rolled away, the pious women with their sacred gifts, the appearance of the angel, the words "He is risen," the weeping of Mary, the meeting with her Lord, the message to the disciples, the joy of the believers, the wild excitement at Jerusalem. What more dramatic descriptions than those of the meetings with the disciples, the walk to Emmaus, the benediction of peace, the assurance to Thomas, the seaside love-feast, and the five hundred assembled upon a Galilean mount? When the apostles stood before kings, their testimony was that Christ rose from the dead. In the presence of heathen congregations they preached Jesus and the resurrection.

They had known "the power of his resurrection," and they made it a power in all their ministry. If missionaries become a power in China, it will be because they preach that Jesus is risen, in a land of idols who once were living men, but now sleep in the silence of the tomb. We can point to the empty sepulchre and cry, "Behold where they laid him."

Jesus "became the first fruits of them that slept." When Paul preached his powerful sermon at Athens, men listened with rapt attention while he discoursed upon idols and the worship of the Creator; but when "they heard of the resurrection from the dead, some mocked." There is a similar experience with the Chinese, for, no matter how solemn is the appeal, when this subject is mentioned the people invariably laugh. To them the idea is so weird and romantic that it sounds like the most extravagant fairy story. So dense is the population, changing every thirty years, the grave mounds leveled by the hand of time to become the resting-places of another retiring generation, the hillsides and the plains filled with graves, that China has been termed "one vast graveyard." It is a city of the dead. That all who sleep in the graves shall arise, and that the sea shall give up the dead who are in it, seems impossible! It is a wonderful doctrine to the pagan; there is nothing like it in heathen literature. It cuts away the flimsy hopes of transmigration, and makes void, even to this ancestor-adoring people, the idolatrous ceremonies after death.

In the Apostles' Creed this is placed as a fundamental truth which must be accepted by every one who professes faith in Christ. It must be frequently and fearlessly proclaimed. It awakes the nation from the dread sleep of superstition and death to hear the voice of the archangel and the trump of God, and to realize that there shall be "a resurrection of the dead, both of the just and the unjust"; "they that have done good, unto the resurrection of life; and they that have done evil, unto the resurrection of damnation." Oh! the sorrow of those who "awake to shame and everlasting contempt," and the blessedness of the righteous who put on incorruption and immortality!

The Scriptures (Matt. xxiv. 3, 29-31; 1 Thess. iv. 15-17; 2 Thess. i. 7-10; Rev. xx. 11-13, and other places) seem to connect with the two great events mentioned above

The Judgment Day.

The types of the judgment in natural religion are abundant, for here the Gentiles "shew the work of the law written in their hearts." They consider that all men go before the king of Tartarus to receive their just reward, so there is "a fearful looking for of judgment." The ancient custom of settling accounts on the last night of the year, and the pursuit of the luckless debtor till the day dawns, tells of a day of final accounts. The large abacus in the temple reminds the people that good and evil are to be summed up at last. No human tongue can depict the scenes of the last day, when the great assembly of men of all ages, all nations, all races, all conditions, all tongues, meet and stand before the Son of man, to whom is committed all judgment; for "we must all appear before the judgment-seat of Christ." The particularity of the day of assizes, when each individual shall appear, the universality of the tribunal, when every act shall be judged, the transparency of the decisions, when secret things shall be made manifest, the separation of the sheep from the goats, make the heathen tremble as they view the day for which all other days were made. They have a symbol of its terrors in the Great Bore in Hangchow Bay on the 18th of the eighth moon, when the white line in the dim distance is soon seen to be an advancing wall of water, maddened in its wild fury as it rushes impetuously forward, roaring as if the elements were dissolved, gurgling and foaming in whirlpools and eddies as it comes thundering along, when, lo! a mountain billow, driven by the opposing shore, comes rolling athwart the advancing wave, and the two, uniting, rush by the spectator, who stands in awe at the magnificent spectacle! But what is this to the truths revealed to us concerning the Judgment Day, when men shall cry "to the mountains and rocks, Fall on us, and hide us from the face of him that sitteth on the throne, and from the wrath of the Lamb; for the great day of his wrath is come"? Then men shall see "a new heaven and a new earth, for the first heaven and the first earth," which idolatrous China so long worshipped, will have "passed away."

CHAPTER XVII.

The Reaper and His Rewards.

THERE is no doctrine so incomprehensible to the Christian as that of rewards; it is one of the mysteries of redemption. The believer feels that the pardon of sin and admittance to heaven is enough, and that it is wondrous grace bestowed upon sinful man which secures to him such benefits as these. But that the Master will reward each act performed in his name and for his sake is what the believer cannot understand. Christ tells of the surprise of the righteous: "Lord, when saw we thee an hungered, and fed thee? or thirsty, and gave thee drink? When saw we thee a stranger, and took thee in? or naked, and clothed thee? Or when saw we thee sick, or in prison, and came unto thee?" Though it seems too good to be true, yet it is a fact, that those on the right hand shall hear the King saying, "Come, ye blessed of my Father, inherit the kingdom prepared for you from the foundation of the world."

In the parable, to the one whose pound gained ten, the nobleman said, "Well, thou good servant, because thou hast been faithful in a very little, have thou authority over ten cities"; and in the parable of the talents, "His lord said unto him, Well done, thou good and faithful servant: thou hast been faithful over a few things, I will make thee ruler over many things: enter thou into the joy of thy lord." The rule of awards is, "For unto every one that hath shall be given, and he shall have abundance." In another parable it is said, "So, when even was come, the lord of the vineyard saith unto his steward, Call the laborers, and give them their hire."

Christ gives a special promise of temporal blessings, and there is no one who has obeyed his parting command who cannot testify, "He is faithful that promised." "And Jesus answered and said, Verily I say unto you, There is no man that hath left house, or brethren, or sisters, or father, or mother, or wife, or children, or lands, for my sake and the gospel's, but he shall receive an hundredfold now in this time" (a special enumeration in the plural number), "houses, and brethren, and sisters, and mothers, and children, and lands, with persecutions, and in the world to come eternal life."

After the Saviour had preached to the Samaritan woman, his disciples returned with the purchased food, and he, sitting beside the well, in view of Mount Ebal and Mount Gerizim, said to them, "Say not ye, There are yet four months, and then cometh harvest?" (a long time before China is converted), "behold, I say unto you, Lift up your eyes, and look on the fields; for they are white already to harvest. And he that reapeth receiveth wages, and gathereth fruit unto life eternal: that both he that soweth and he that reapeth may rejoice together;" that is, there is as much joy in sowing as in reaping. The Master continued his discourse: "And herein is that saying true, One soweth, and another reapeth. I sent you to reap that whereon ye bestowed no labor: other men labored, and ye are entered into their labors." Prophets and kings had labored with the Jews. These words were not spoken to missionaries to the heathen, for those who perform the work of preparation, as David did for Solomon's temple, have not gone before them.

Isaiah said, "Blessed are ye that sow beside all waters." David sang, "They that sow in tears shall reap in joy. He that goeth forth and weepeth, bearing precious seed, shall doubtless come again with rejoicing, bringing his sheaves with him." Paul wrote, "He which soweth bountifully shall reap also bountifully"; "He that soweth to the Spirit shall of the Spirit reap life everlasting. And let us not be weary in well-doing:

for in due season we shall reap, if we faint not." In a fruitful year the Chinese plant one grain of rice, and at the harvest there are on the one head one hundred grains; so the spiritual harvest will be thirty, sixty, and one hundred-fold.

The sower is the preacher: "And I saw another angel fly in the midst of heaven, having the everlasting gospel to preach to them that dwell on the earth, and to every nation, and kindred, and tongue, and people." "And this gospel of the kingdom shall be preached in all the world, for a witness unto all nations." And with what result? "Many shall run to and fro, and knowledge shall be increased." "And they shall teach no more every man his neighbor, and every man his brother, saying, Know the Lord: for they shall all know me, from the least of them unto the greatest of them, saith the Lord." "For the earth shall be full of the knowledge of the glory of the Lord, as the waters cover the sea." Besides the many prophecies about the kingdom to cheer the church, in her arduous labors in China a special promise is given: "Behold, these shall come from far: and, lo! these from the north and from the west; and these from the land of Sinim."

In view of the advent of Messiah, the prophet exclaimed, "Behold, his reward is with him"; and from heaven his own voice was heard, "Behold, I come quickly, and my reward is with me." If Christ does not forget the handing of a cup of cold water to a disciple, and will in no wise let the giver lose his reward, how much more will he remember those who bring the water of life to the multitudes who perish with thirst! The Master told his disciples of the great value of one soul. The apostle to the Gentiles said, "I am made all things to all men, that I might by all means save some." James closes his epistle with this cheering exhortation: "Let him know, that he which converteth the sinner from the error of his way shall save a soul from death, and shall hide a multitude of sins." Ministers are stars in the right hand of him who walks in the midst of the golden candlesticks; and in the resurrection "one star differeth from another star in glory," but all shine brightly. The prophet said, "They that be wise shall shine as the brightness of the firmament; and they that turn many to righteousness, as the stars, for ever and ever." Therefore, the laborer may feel assured of the "crown of righteousness" laid up for him in heaven, and at "that day" to be placed on his head; and that it will be granted to him to sit with Jesus on his throne, even as he also overcame, and is set down with his Father on his throne.

www.ingramcontent.com/pod-product-compliance
Lightning Source LLC
Chambersburg PA
CBHW031742230426
43669CB00007B/442